# SUSHMA SWARAJ
## THE PEOPLE'S MINISTER

Sushmita Dutta

Pharos Books

**ISBN: 978-93-90697-06-9**
**eISBN: 978-93-90697-14-4**



**Publisher**: **Pharos Books (P) Ltd.**
Plot No.-55, Main Mother Dairy Road
Pandav Nagar, East Delhi-110092
**Phone**: 011-40395855
**WhatsApp:** +91 8447931000
**E-mail**: sales@pharosbooks.in
**Website**: www.pharosbooks.in
**Edition:** 2021
**Cover Design:** Virendra Singh Bhandari
**Inner Design:** Surendra Kumar
**Printed By:** Sushma Book Binding House, Okhla Industrial Area, Phase II, New Delhi-110020

**Sushma Swaraj: The People's Minister**
**Author:** Sushmita Dutta

# Introduction

**Sushma Swaraj** (1952-2019), served as the Minister of External Affairs from May 26, 2014 to May 30, 2019. Her demise on 6 August, 2019 left the whole country in a state of shock and distress. Known as a firebrand leader and political stalwart of the Bharatiya Janata Party (BJP), she was one of the rare politicians who was loved and admired by everyone irrespective of their political views.

She used social media not merely as an outreach tool, but as an effective virtual "darbar." She didn't just lend her voice to Twitter—she made it the instrument for the voiceless. Working round the clock to save Indians in distress, she once famously said "I do not sleep" and "I do not let Indian envoys sleep."

# Contents

# Chapter-1

## Birth and Parentage

Sushma Swaraj was born on February 14, 1952 in a middle-class family at Ambala Cantonment, in Haryana. She was born to Shri Hardev Sharma and Shrimati Laxmi Devi. Her parents hailed from Dharampura area in Lahore, Pakistan. Her father, Hardev Sharma, was a prominent member in the Rashtriya Swayamsevak Sangh (RSS), a pro-Hindu organization, of which the BJP is an offshoot.

(Zee News)

**Early childhood days in Ambala**

❑

# Chapter-2

## Early Life and Education

She graduated from Sanatan Dharma College, in Ambala Cantonment, Haryana and got her bachelor's degree with honours in Political Science and Sanskrit. In 1970, she received the **Best Student Award** from SD College, in Ambala, Haryana. For three consecutive years, she won the title of **Best Cadet of NCC.** She also won the **Best Hindi Speaker Award** in a state-level competition held by the Language Department of Haryana continuously for three years.

(Zee News)

**Best Cadet of NCC**

After that, she pursued a degree course in LLB from the Department of Laws of the Punjab University in Chandigarh. At Punjab University, she was declared the **Best Speaker in Hindi** at the AC Bali Memorial Declamation Contest. She was also awarded the university colour there. She was the president of **Hindi Sahitya Sammelan** of the state of Haryana for four years.

Apart from academics, Sushma Swaraj was excellent in extracurricular activities. She received various awards of distinction in debates, recitations, rhetoric contests, dramas and other cultural activities. Besides being a keen reader of poetry and literature, she also took interest in classical music, poetry, fine arts and drama.

### Ambala recalls Sushma Swaraj's childhood days

*(India Today, 2019)*

A family living in Ambala Cantonment's BC Bazaar area recalled: "Right from her childhood, she was fond of taking part in debates and contests in school."

**Shyam Bihari,** an elderly man who lived in the same neighbourhood, told reporters after the news of the BJP leader's death on Tuesday night came in: "From Class 6, she had shown an inclination towards politics and later she realised what she had aimed for. She was very affectionate, caring and ever ready to help. To render help to any genuine person who was in need, she did not care even if he was a supporter of a rival political party," he said.

Another man, now in his 60s, recalled that Sushma Swaraj used to fetch milk for her family in the morning, around the time he and his friends played cricket in the neighbourhood. "At times, the cricket ball would hit the pail, spilling the milk. But Sushmaji never got angry at us and always used to tell us to continue playing," he said.

**Gauri,** a domestic help at the house, was inconsolable on hearing about her death. "She was very nice. She had come here a few months ago. When she learnt that I had two daughters, she told me to give them a good education and offered any help that might be needed from her side to ensure that they got the best facilities," she said.

"We used to call Sushmaji **'buaji.'** I am deeply saddened at her death. At the same time, I am also proud of the fact that she rose to such heights in her life and became a role model for millions," she said.

## How Did She Enter Politics?

Considered as the leader of the next generation, her inception in Indian politics was as a student leader in 1970. Many protests against the government of Indira Gandhi were organised by her. She was an exceptional speaker and campaigner, who, after joining the Janata Party, got actively involved in campaigning against the Emergency. Her quest in Indian politics saw her as the **first woman Chief Minister of Delhi** and later as the **first woman Leader of Opposition.**

❑

# Chapter-3

## Political Career

In 1973, she started practicing as a lawyer in the Supreme Court of India. Here, she met her future husband, Swaraj Kaushal, who was closely associated with the socialist leader, George Fernandes. Later, she became a part of George Fernandes's legal defence team in 1975. She actively participated in Jayaprakash Narayan's **Total Revolution Movement.** After the Emergency, she joined the Bharatiya Janata Party. Her calibre and achievements were soon recognized by the party as a result of which she became a national leader.

## Early Political Career

Sushma Swaraj began her political career in 1970 when she joined the Akhil Bhartiya Vidyarthi Parishad (ABVP), an active student's wing of

(India Times)

the RSS. She was also an active member in the Rashtriya Swayamsevak Sangh (RSS).

## State-Level Politics

She became a member of the Haryana Legislative Assembly from 1977 to 1982, after winning the Ambala Cantonment assembly seat. In July 1977, she was sworn in as the Cabinet Minister in the Janata Party Government headed by the then Chief Minister, Devi Lal. She became the **youngest Cabinet Minister** in India at the age of 25 and held eight portfolios from 1977 to 1979, which included Social Welfare, Labour and Employment.

In the assembly elections of 1977, she had won the Ambala Cantonment seat with nearly 64 per cent votes, double that of her closest rival. She went on to serve two more terms in the legislative assembly, in 1977-82 and 1987-90.

In 1979, she became the Janata Party's State President in Haryana, a position she held for four years. In 1984, Sushma Swaraj joined the Bharatiya Janata Party (BJP) and was eventually appointed as the secretary of the party. She held the position of the **All India Secretary** of the party for two years. She played a key role in strengthening the BJP across the country through the 1990s.

(DNA India)

In 1987, Sushma Swaraj was re-elected from the Haryana Legislative Assembly. This time again she became the Cabinet Minister holding the portfolios of Civil Supplies, Food and Education from 1987 to 1990.

## National-Level Politics

In April 1990, Sushma Swaraj was elected as a member of the Rajya Sabha and remained there until she was elected to the 11th Lok Sabha from South Delhi constituency in 1996. In the same year, during the thirteen-day government under the leadership of Atal Bihari Vajpayee, she served as the Union Minister for Information and Broadcasting. She took a revolutionary step of live telecasting Lok Sabha debates.

### Her Fiery Speech of 1996

On June 11, 1996 Sushma Swaraj, while making her most impassioned speech on the floor of the Lok Sabha talked about the Bharatiya Janata Party's (BJP) long-term plan of repealing Article 370 from Jammu and Kashmir.

Twenty-three summers later, the senior BJP leader expressed her gratitude to Prime Minister Narendra Modi for revoking the same article, in her last tweet hours before she breathed her last.

"@narendramodi ji - Thank you Prime Minister. Thank you very much. I was waiting to see this day in my lifetime," she wrote moments before she was taken to AIIMS, Delhi, after suffering a massive heart attack, where she was declared dead.

In the 1996 speech in Parliament she stood for speaking against the no-confidence motion. She lashed out at her political opponents after Atal Bihari Vajpayee had to resign from the Prime Minister's post.

**"We are communal, because we want to abolish the Article 370, we are communal, because we want to put an end to discrimination based on caste and creed in this country...**

**Mr Speaker, we are communal, because we want the voices of the Kashmiri refugees to be heard,"** she said.

Amid a roaring House, Sushma Swaraj laid the foundation for what would go on to be one of the most landmark decisions taken by any government of the country since Independence. Later in her speech, the former External Affairs Minister went on to explain why the BJP had to step down and equated her analogies to the Ramayana and the Mahabharata.

"When one Manthara and one Shakuni can keep the likes of Lord Rama and Yudishthir out of their right to rule, then if you take a look around this House, you'll find many Mantharas and many Shakunis opposing us. How can we stay in power? I suppose it (no-confidence motion) is the nature of Ramrajya and Surajya," she said.

Her speech gathered such enthusiastic response from the members of the House that the then speaker, PA Sangma had to intervene. He said, "Please, don't make your speech so interesting!"

❑

# Chapter-4

## Union Minister of Information & Broadcasting (1998)

She was re-elected to the 12th Lok Sabha from South Delhi Parliamentary Constituency for a second term in March 1998. Under the second term of Atal Bihari Vajpayee Government, she was sworn in as Union Cabinet Minister for Information and Broadcasting with additional charge of the Ministry of Telecommunications from 19 March, 1998 to 2 October, 1998.

(Business Standard)

Under her ministership, she started community radio at universities and other institutions. The most notable decision she made came in the form of giving film production an "industry" status. This decision to declare film production as an industry made the Indian film industry eligible for bank financing, thereby removing dubious sources of money and offered a chance of loans with reduced interest rates. According to an *India Today* report from 1998, around 25 per cent of films at that time were financed by moneylenders, who lent money at huge interest rates of 36-40 per cent per annum. Apart from that, 70 per cent films were produced by businessman, including builders, jewellers, traders and around 5 per cent from the underworld.

As a result of her significant contribution to the entertainment industry, celebrities were in extreme grief when they heard about the untimely demise of the former External Affairs Minister, Sushma Swaraj. Former BJP MP, Dharmendra, current Members of Parliament, Hema Malini and Sunny Deol, Union Minister, Babul Supriyo and MPs, Manoj Tiwari, Ravi Kishan, Kirron Kher, and leader Jaya Prada were among those who shared their grief of the veteran leader's loss.

Tributes poured in for Sushma Swaraj from several Bollywood celebrities, who were devastated by the tragic news.

## Emotional Tributes

**Dharmendra** shared that she used to taunt him for leaving politics but would give him a tight embrace and added that she was India's great leader, everyone's favourite and his younger sister. He prayed that her soul rests in peace.

**Shabana Azmi** remembered that historical moment in her tweets of condolence for Sushma Swaraj. She wrote: "Deeply saddened that Sushma Swaraj has passed away. In spite of political differences, we had an extremely cordial relationship. I was 1 of her Navratans as she called us during her Information and Broadcasting ministership and she gave industry status to film. Articulate sharp and accessible. RIP."

**Parineeti Chopra** wrote that she was inspired by the leader on a personal level. "I hail from Ambala Cantt, same as Sushma Swarajji. Always felt proud that a woman from our small town made it big, and made a difference. Sushmaji rest in peace. You inspired me on a personal level."

**Vivek Oberoi** wrote: "An Iron Lady who was not only a true patriot but an incredible inspiration for each and every one of us. An epitome of women empowerment and leadership. #SushmaSwarajji you will be missed and remembered forever. My deepest condolences and prayers to the family."

**Lata Mangeshkar** wrote: "Deeply shocked and saddened to hear about Sushma Swarajji's sudden demise. A graceful and honest leader, a sensitive and selfless soul, a keen understanding of music and poetry and a dear friend. Our former external minister will be remembered fondly."

**Javed Akhtar** wrote: "Deeply saddened by Sushmaji's demise. The Music Fraternity will be indebted to her for magnificent defence of their rights in the Lok Sabha. You were an exceptional person Sushmaji. We will always remain thankful to you."

❑

# Chapter-5

## Chief Minister of Delhi (1998)

However, one of the most turbulent phases of her illustrious political career was her stint as the Delhi Chief Minister. Sushma Swaraj assumed office as the Chief Minister of Delhi on October 12, 1998. Her elevation to the coveted post triggered a wave of criticism from political rivals who even went to the extent of claiming that BJP MLAs were summoned at the party headquarters in Delhi and were "forced to vote" in favour of her against the incumbent Chief Minister, Sahib Singh Verma. Political circles even assumed that the party's top leadership, including former Chief Minister, Madanlal Khurana were irked by her promotion to the top job.

(Business Standard)

**Sushma Swaraj Taking Oath as Delhi CM**

In 1998, she became Delhi's first woman Chief Minister, though only for 52 days. But even during that brief stint, Sushma Swaraj worked as if she was on a "mission" and did "firefighting" for the BJP. At that time, an MP from South Delhi, she was appointed as Chief Minister on October 12, 1998 just months before the assembly elections in Delhi. She took charge from late Sahib Singh Verma, who served as the Chief Minister for two-and-a-half years.

## Reason for her selection as Delhi Chief Minister

Sushma Swaraj's appointment was a desperate attempt to salvage the deteriorating situation just months before the assembly elections. The then BJP-led government under Sahib Singh Verma had come under sharp criticism as it was unable to curb the prices of onions, which was fast becoming a serious issue. The party was also unable to address the demand for auto-rickshaw fare revision, and complaints of shortage of electricity, especially in unauthorised colonies had been increasing. The party required a new face to counter anti-incumbency.

Sahib Singh Verma was also engaged in a violent disagreement with his predecessor late Madan Lal Khurana, who had to quit, following the allegations of corruption, after his name appeared in the Hawala scam. After Khurana got a clean chit from the courts, he staked claim to chief ministership but Sahib Singh refused to relinquish the post.

This created an impression that the party was unable to govern Delhi. Sheila Dikshit, who was head of Congress's Delhi unit, was actively taking on the BJP government, holding protests against the onion prices. "Elections were approaching. It was felt that a new face, especially a woman, would help the party. Sushma Swaraj then an MP from Delhi," said Rajya Sabha MP Vijay Goel, who worked with her twice in NDA-led government in 1999 and 2014.

## As Delhi Chief Minister

In her brief stint, she wasted no time in shifting her focus to the city of Delhi. Contrary to critics who made public statements about her political roots in Haryana and her non-familiarity with the ways of Lutyen's city, she immediately fitted into the portfolio. She formed a special committee to restore the supply of onions. She even ordered setting up of vans for distribution of onions.

Those who worked with her recall how she carried out surprise inspections, especially at police stations, at night. BJP leader, Ved Vyas Mahajan said: "Police was not under the CM, but she would carry out inspections at police stations to see if they were working to address the problems of the people."

One such incident which was widely reported in domestic publications was her visit to the Kalyanpuri police station in East Delhi. She reportedly went to the police station in a private car without her elaborate security cover. Upon noticing that the station-house officer (SHO) was not present at his desk, she waited for two whole hours before pulling up the top brass of the Delhi Police over the absence of the officer responsible for keeping peace in a crime-infested area. The SHO was suspended with immediate effect and the furious Chief Minister even wrote a note to the Home Minister, demanding action against errant officers. (As narrated by Anuradha Raman in *The Pioneer* on October 18, 1998.)

However, Mrs. Swaraj's efforts did not succeed. "It was too late by then, as the public had made up its mind to vote BJP out. But she worked as if she was on a mission and tried to control the situation. She would carry out inspections at government offices to ensure that officials were working."

Omesh Saigal, the chief secretary in Sushma Swaraj's government, said: "She had to grapple with a lot of issues. During her brief stint, she was fighting control price of onions due to the commodity's shortage. But she had very little time to make any significant impact."

Her rapport with the bureaucracy played a vital role in her nearly two-month tenure. Jagdish Mukhi, governor of Assam and Mizoram (Additional charge), who was then finance minister, said: "She was a very forward looking, positive and open to new ideas. She took the bureaucracy in confidence while working in the Delhi government."

SK Sharma, former Delhi assembly secretary, said Sushma Swaraj did not call any session of the Assembly since she did not get enough time. Sharma said, she decided to resign as MLA from Hauz Khas to continue as MP from South Delhi after the BJP lost the 1998 assembly elections.

As the Chief Minister of Delhi for 52 days, Sushma Swaraj managed to gain a stoic reputation as an effective administrator. Her campaign to improve the law and order situation in the national capital captured many-a-headlines back in the day. She often made impromptu visits to police stations and reprimanded officers for deviating from their duties. It is to be noted that she decided to conduct impromptu checks while leaving her security cover at a time when top political leaders in Delhi were under constant threats following the murder of Ved Singh, a Samata Party candidate from Nangloi Jat Assembly constituency.

She resigned from her position in December 3, 1998 the same year.

❑

# Chapter-6

## Remembering an Iconic Campaign

The high-voltage election contest between BJP's Sushma Swaraj and Congress leader Sonia Gandhi in the 1999 Lok Sabha elections brought the Bellary constituency to national limelight. Though she lost the election, she weaved an emotional connect with Bellary and helped BJP lay its base in Karnataka. Her followers in the constituency remember her as Sushma 'thayi' (mother in Kannada).

(Deccan Herald)

**Sushma Swaraj vs Sonia Gandhi**

It all started in 1999, when Sonia Gandhi contested the Lok Sabha elections. She filed her nomination from two constituencies—Bellary, Karnataka, and the Gandhi family seat of Amethi in Uttar Pradesh. The Bharatiya Janata Party (BJP) nominated Sushma Swaraj to contest against Mrs. Gandhi portraying her as the **"adarsh bharatiya nari"**—an ideal Indian woman. With a big bindi on her forehead, sindoor (red vermilion powder) in the parting of her hairline and dressed in traditional attire, she was the perfect nationalistic foil to what the BJP ridiculed as the "Italian-born" Gandhi, widow of former Prime Minister, Rajiv Gandhi. And thus, the seeds of the battle between the "Indian beti" and the "foreign bahu"—daughter of India versus Italian daughter-in-law—were sown.

However, Sushma Swaraj lost in Bellary, and subsequently, the Congress Party came to power in the state. Sonia Gandhi won the election with a margin of 56,100 votes. But the battle was revived in 2004, when the United Progressive Alliance (UPA) won the general election and Congress loyalists urged Sonia Gandhi to take up the prime ministership.

Then, in what can be described as an emotional outburst, Mrs. Swaraj threatened to shave her head and wear white—a Hindu sign of mourning—eat groundnuts and sleep on the floor if Sonia Gandhi became the Prime Minister. At that time, she had said her reaction was due to her hurt sentiments because, as she put it, "even after the culmination of British rule and the sacrifices made by fellow Indians...a foreigner was being chosen." She maintained this line ever since, expressing admiration for Sonia Gandhi on one hand but stating that her selection for the top job was unacceptable to her.

The tables were turned when Sonia Gandhi refused to accept the post of prime minister. With the **bahu** making the ultimate Indian woman's sacrifice, the entire game changed. A political analyst, who did not wish to be identified said: "The BJP could not keep harping on her foreign origins after that. Whether it was an emotional decision or a calculated one, we can only speculate, but it silenced all of Sonia's critics and ended the foreign aspect of the debate once and for all."

## When Sushma Swaraj's Kannada speech at Bellary election surprised everyone

Sushma Swaraj was nominated from Bellary by the BJP against Congress leader Sonia Gandhi. Though Sushma lost the battle, her fiery speech at Bellary was what propelled her as a prominent leader of the BJP.

Her four-minute speech received thunderous applause from the crowd that gathered at the rally. Even former Prime Minister, Atal Bihari Vajpayee, who was at the rally was awestruck by Sushma Swaraj's fluency in Kannada.

Her connection with Bellary did not stop after the 1999 Lok Sabha elections, as Sushma used to visit Bellary every year for the Varamahalakshmi festival. This continued for about 11 years. The festival would be celebrated in the house of BK Srinivasa Murthy. And following the puja, they would then proceed to the mass marriage organised by her 'adopted son' Sriramulu of BJP where she would be the Chief Guest.

## Bellary Remembers Sushma Swaraj

Recalling her association with the district in north-west Karnataka, former Chief Minister Jagadish Shettar, said: "She is a daughter of Karnataka and also she was very proficient in Kannada. Following the instruction of the party Sushma had contested the election in Bellary against Sonia Gandhi. Though she lost the election but it helped the BJP create a strong base in Bellary and also in Karnataka. Whenever we were meeting her, she would address us in Kannada."

Sushma Swaraj learnt Kannada when she was lodged in Bangalore Central Jail after the Emergency was declared. This helped her in reaching out to voters during election campaigns. She addressed her rallies in Kannada which impressed voters in the state. "She not only knew Kannada, she even was a keen observer of Karnataka politics," said Jagadish Shettar.

❑

# Chapter-7

## Minister of Information and Broadcasting (2000-2003)

She returned to Parliament in April 2000 as a Rajya Sabha member from Uttar Pradesh. She was reallocated to Uttarakhand when the new state was carved out of Uttar Pradesh on 9 November, 2000. She was sworn in the Cabinet as the Union Minister for Information and Broadcasting, a position she held from September 2000 until January 2003.

(Rajya Sabha TV)

**CAS Bill Passed Unanimously in Rajya Sabha**

### CAS Bill passed unanimously in Rajya Sabha

On 10 December, 2002 Sushma Swaraj pulled out another ace from her sleeve, getting one of her favourite subjects—the introduction of the Conditional Access System Bill—passed by one of the Houses of Indian Parliament with minimum of fuss and, surprisingly, overwhelming support.

Now, consumers will have to pay for only those channels which he wishes to see. The maximum price for the basic tier of service comprising free to air channels would be determined by the government.

CEO Kunal Dasgupta of Sony Entertainment Television India said: "We welcome the passage of the Bill and we hope to work closely with the government in the implementation process."

Talking on behalf of the cable industry HTMT's executive V-P corporate, Ashok Mansukhani said: "We are very happy that the Bill has been passed. We'll work very hard in conjunction with broadcasters to bring even more channels at an affordable cost within the next six months."

❑

# Chapter-8

## Minister of Health and Family Welfare, Parliamentary Affairs (2003-2004)

She was Minister of Health, Family Welfare and Parliamentary Affairs from January 2003 until May 2004, when the National Democratic Alliance (NDA) Government lost the general election. As Union Health Minister, she set up six **All India Institute of Medical Sciences** at Bhopal (MP), Bhubaneshwar (Odisha), Jodhpur (Rajasthan), Patna (Bihar), Raipur (Chhattisgarh) and Rishikesh (Uttarakhand).

She was re-elected to the Rajya Sabha for the third term in April 2006 from Madhya Pradesh state. She served as the Leader of Opposition in Rajya Sabha till April 2009.

(Wikimedia Commons)

**Smt. Sushma Swaraj meets a delegation led by the Minister of State for Health and Transport of Singapore, Dr. Balaji Sadasivan in New Delhi on January 9, 2004**

❑

# Chapter-9

## Leader of the Opposition (2009-2014)

She won the 2009 election for the 15th Lok Sabha from the Vidisha Lok Sabha constituency in Madhya Pradesh by a record margin of over 400,000 votes. Sushma Swaraj became the Leader of the Opposition in the 15th Lok Sabha in place of Lal Krishna Advani on 21 December, 2009 and retained this position till May 2014 when in 2014 general election her party got a major victory.

Deccan Herald

## Sushma Swaraj should have been Prime Minister in 2014

In a newspaper article written by Congress leader and former Union Minister P Chidambaram, Sushma Swaraj was the "natural choice" to Prime Minister's post in 2014. "During 2009-2014, she (Sushma) was the leader of the Opposition in the Lok Sabha, a position that in a parliamentary democracy should have made her the natural choice to be the prime minister if her party won the election."

"The BJP won the election in 2014, but an "outsider" with tremendous energy and political skill had already stormed his way to become the leader of the party and, therefore, Prime Minister," wrote Mr Chidambaram on Mr Narendra Modi.

After the election, he said although Ms Swaraj became Minister of External Affairs, she had "little say in the conduct of foreign policy"---as this had been taken over by the Prime Minister's Office.

"The smart Ms Swaraj invented a role for herself---champion of the little person who was stranded in a foreign country or had been abducted/imprisoned or denied a passport/visa or required admission to an Indian university/hospital and so on," said the Congress leader. He further said, "there was a need for such a Good Samaritan and the people seemed to love her benevolence."

"It also helped that she (Sushma) scrupulously avoided confrontation with opposition parties."

❑

# Chapter-10

## Minister of External Affairs (2014-2019)

Smt. Sushma Swaraj served as the Minister of External Affairs under Prime Minister Narendra Modi from May 2014-May 2019. She was responsible for implementing the foreign policy of Narendra Modi. She was also the second woman to hold this position after Indira Gandhi.

### Key policy decisions

#### Fast-track Diplomacy

The Prime Minister, along with Sushma Swaraj, spent the first day at work meeting leaders of the SAARC nations and Mauritius. This signified the priority placed by the new government on strengthening the bonds of friendship and development in India's South Asian neighbourhood.

#### Foreign trips made as External Affairs Minister

The following is a list of international visits made by Sushma Swaraj after taking office as External Affairs Minister on 26 May, 2014.

**Bangladesh:** Her visit to Bangladesh on June 25-27, 2014 marked an "excellent beginning" in addressing the mutual concerns in the spirit of good neighbourliness. It laid emphasis on comprehensive and equitable partnership, mutually beneficial relations, youth-led development, people-to-people contact, and interlinkages to move forward in South Asia.

**Nepal:** Prior to Narendra Modi's visit, she made a three-day visit to Nepal from 27 July–29 July 2014 and co-chaired the Indo-Nepal Joint Commission meeting. She also prepared the ground for PM Modi's scheduled visit. The last visit by a foreign minister of India to Nepal was made 23 years ago.

**Afghanistan:** She arrived in Kabul on 10 September to hold discussions with President Hamid Karzai. The main agenda of her visit was to strengthen the Indo-Afghan strategic security cooperation following NATO withdrawal from the country by end of 2014 and re-emergence of the Taliban and other al-Qaeda in the subcontinent. She also inaugurated a new Chancery complex in Kabul.

**Tajikistan:** On 11–12 September, she visited Dushanbe, Tajikistan to attend the 13th annual summit of the Shanghai Cooperation Organization, which is often regarded by the West as a counter organisation of NATO, where India so far held an observer status. But from Dushanbe summit, India was formerly granted a full membership so that if everything went well, PM Modi could participate at the heads of government summit in Astana, Kazakhstan in December.

**Mauritius:** She made a three-day visit from 1-3 November, to celebrate Aapravasi Divas, marking 180 years since the first Indian indentured labourers arrived in Mauritius. She called on the President, Rajkeswur Purryag and Prime Minister, Dr Navinchandra Ramgoolam to discuss bilateral and regional issues of common interest, particularly to talk on cooperation between Indian Navy and Mauritian Coast Guard to ensure the safety and security of the Indian Ocean region.

**United Arab Emirates:** During her maiden trip to Abu Dhabi on 10–12 November she tried to win the confidence of potential UAE investors and welcomed them to join the new Indian Government efforts to build world class infrastructure in India. She also held discussions with Sheikh Abdullah bin Zayed Al Nahyan.

**South Korea:** She visited South Korea on 28–30 December to attend the 7th Joint-Commission meeting in Seoul. Trade and investments to top the agenda included joint shipbuilding ventures under **Make in India** programme.

On completion of the first 100 days of the first Narendra Modi government, the External Affairs Ministry published a booklet called **Fast Track Diplomacy** showcasing its achievements. During her tenure she had said that "fast-track diplomacy" had three faces – proactive, strong and sensitive. Thereafter, she held round-table meetings with all Indian heads of missions to the SAARC region, ASEAN region, and West Asia separately as a follow-up measure.

## Multilateral Engagements

### Act East Policy

The visits of the External Affairs Minister, Smt. Sushma Swaraj to Myanmar, Vietnam and Singapore took India's ties with the East to a new phase, from **'Look East'** to **'Act East.'**

The NDA government in 2014 came to power with a clear view to focus on improving relationships with ASEAN and other East Asian countries as per India's **'Look East policy'** which was formulated during PV Narasimha Rao's government in 1992 for better economic engagement with India's eastern neighbours. However, she stressed on the need for an **'Act East Policy'** that she said would replace the **'Look East Policy'** emphasising a more proactive role for India in the region.

**Myanmar:** She visited Nay Pyi Taw, the modern capital of Myanmar (Burma) for the India-ASEAN Foreign Ministers' Meeting, EAS Foreign Ministers' Meeting and ASEAN Regional Forum (ARF) Meeting. She held bilateral meetings with her counterparts from 11 countries, including Australia, Brunei Darussalam, Canada, China, Indonesia, Japan, Myanmar, New Zealand, South Korea, Thailand and Vietnam. The main things discussed were connectivity projects, including land, maritime and air connectivity, and the much-awaited trilateral highway, which will connect India-Myanmar-Thailand.

**Vietnam:** She travelled to Vietnam to discuss India's plan to ramp up its engagement in the oil sector and deepen defence ties.

**Singapore:** In Singapore, she called on Prime Minister, Lee Hsien Loong regarding Singapore's investment in India and their potential role in PM Modi's pet "smart city" project. She also met her counterpart, Mr K Shanmugam and inaugurated the 'Year of India' celebration to commemorate the 50th anniversary of the establishment of diplomatic relations between India and Singapore.

She invited partnership of the Singaporean companies to speed up connectivity and infrastructure projects in India, particularly, along the Delhi-Mumbai Industrial Corridor (DMIC), the Chennai-Bangalore Industrial Corridor and the North East of India.

**North East:** She decided to set up New Passport Seva Kendras in the North East including Shillong, Imphal, Itanagar, Agartala, Kohima and Gangtok.

❑

# Chapter-11

## Years between 2015-2019

**China:** Sushma Swaraj made her maiden visit to the People's Republic of China from 31 January-3 February where she met her counterpart Wang Yi and called on Chinese President Xi Jinping apart from participating in Russia–India–China (RIC) trilateral foreign ministers meeting in Beijing. She inaugurated "visit India" campaign to promote more Chinese tourists in India.

**Turkmenistan**: She visited Ashgabat on 7 April-9 April 2015 on a three-day visit. There she met President Gurbanguly Berdymukhamedov besides co-chairing an inter-governmental joint commission with her counterpart Rashid Meredov. The Turkmenistan-Afghanistan-Pakistan-India (TAPI) gas pipeline was the key agenda of talks between India and Turkmenistan.

**Nepal:** She announced $1 billion aid to rebuild Nepal, that caused widespread destruction caused by an earthquake that occurred on April 25, 2015. The aid was used to rebuild physical infrastructure including schools, roads, hospitals as well as some key heritage sites that were devastated by the earthquake.

### 2016

**Israel:** She paid an official visit to Israel from 17-18 January 2016. This was her first visit to Israel. During her visit, she held discussions with the Israeli leadership and reviewed the entire gamut of India-Israel bilateral relations. The two sides shared firm belief in the values of democracy and free market economy. The two countries also shared close relation in the fields of agriculture, science & technology and education.

**Iran:** She visited Iran on April 18, 2016, which was her first visit to the country as India's External Affairs Minister. Here, she met her Iranian counterpart, Javad Zarif, the Iranian president, Hassan Rouhani, and Iran's supreme leader, Ayatollah Ali Khamenei.

She stressed the desire of India to expand all-round cooperation with Iran particularly in energy, connectivity, ports, infrastructure, trade and culture. She also hoped that the two sides will sign the bilateral contract on Chabahar Port, and also the Trilateral Agreement involving India, Iran and Afghanistan on Trade and Transit Corridor through the Chabahar port.

**BRICS:** On October 15-16, 2016 India hosted the eighth annual Summit of BRICS in Goa. India assumed chairmanship of BRICS (Brazil-Russia-India-China-South Africa) from Russia on February 15. India's core-theme during BRICS chairmanship would be building responsive, inclusive and collective solutions for the grouping. The logo for the Summit was a lotus having colours from all the five member countries and a traditional 'namaste' in the centre.

## 2017

In 2017, she was highly appreciated by fans and critics when she decided to grant a year-long medical visa to a Pakistani girl, Shireen Shiraz for an open-heart surgery. She helped out two more Pakistani nationals the same year by granting them medical visas for carrying out liver surgeries in India. Her humanitarian aid won her praise from political counterparts, both national and international.

## 73rd Session of the UN General Assembly

Sushma Swaraj addressed the 73rd Session of the United Nations General Assembly (UNGA) in New York City on September 29, 2018.

She began her address at the General Assembly first by congratulating Ma Fernanda Espinosa on assuming the position as the President of the 73rd Session of the UNGA. She also recalled that the first woman to

(She The People TV)

**Sushma Swaraj at the 73rd Session of the United Nations General Assembly**

occupy this position was an Indian, Smt. Vijayalakshmi Pandit, in 1953.

Next, she spoke on women empowerment and its importance for a nation's development and growth. She highlighted various schemes, in India, that point towards women's welfare and named the Ujjwala scheme, through which 50 million gas connections have been provided so far. She also spoke about schemes such as Skill Development Programme and Mudra Programme which help in the skill development and help the poor turn into entrepreneurs.

She discussed maternity leave benefits saying that at a time when some developed nations, with huge economies, did not offer more than six weeks paid maternity leave, India is implementing the Maternity Benefit Scheme. This scheme allows women to get 26 weeks of paid leave to care for their newborn.

She told the 193-member UN body that under PM Modi's leadership, India had commenced unmatched economic and social transformation. She stated how through the 'Jan Dhan Yojana' over 320 million Indians would have bank accounts and receive allotments from the government's welfare programmes into their personal accounts, through Direct Benefit Transfer.

She also cited example of 'Ayushmaan Bharat', the world's biggest health insurance programme through which 500 million Indians would benefit from an insurance cover of Rs. 500,000 per family per year. Another scheme she spoke of was India's housing scheme aimed at building nearly 21 million homes by 2022.

She also shared PM Modi's vision of building a 'New India' by 2022. This 'New India', she thought would be 'Swachh Bharat, Swasth Bharat' (Clean India, Healthy India), 'Samarth Bharat, Surakshit Bharat' (Prosperous India, Secure India), 'Shikshit Bharat, Viksit Bharat' (Educated India, Developed India), 'Urjawan Bharat, Shaktiman Bharat' (Energised India, Strong India).

She further said that the biggest challenge came from existential threats of climate change and terrorism. Thus, nations must come together and save the world from adverse effects of climate change. She did not keep away from expressing anger against Pakistan. She adamantly spoke of how the neighbour country glorifies killers and terrorism.

Further, she pressed on the need for the UN to start functioning like a family. She urged for better reforms and quick changes that are required in the Security Council.

She concluded by insisting that the UN General Assembly be made into a platform of understanding, assistance and true justice where nations understand each other's pain and work with developed countries to ease and eliminate this pain. "Arrogance has no place in our scheme of things; arrogance is counter-productive and self-defeating. Let us work for the benefit of the less fortunate. Let us work for a world where there is peace, serenity and shared prosperity; a world that is free from terrorism, tension and violence," she said.

## 2019

However, she did not contest the Lok Sabha 2019 elections and opted out of Prime Minister Narendra Modi's new cabinet, due to health reasons.

❑

# Chapter-12

## Her Contributions and Achievements

While being the Minister of External Affairs of the NDA government, she issued an NOC against a specific query raised by the UK government about the Indo-UK bilateral relationship if the UK granted permission to Lalit Modi, an Indian fugitive in a cricket scandal who had been staying in Britain since 2010, to attend his wife's surgery in Portugal. She conveyed to the British High Commissioner that they should examine Modi's request as per their rules and wrote "if the British government chooses to give travel documents to Lalit Modi—that will not spoil our bilateral relations."

On 12 August 2015, the leader of the Indian National Congress, Mallikarjun Kharge, moved an Adjournment Motion in the Lower House seeking the resignation of Sushma Swaraj due to her alleged conduct in this regard. Initially, the motion was rejected by the Speaker, but it was accepted on her insistence. Intervening in the motion, she clarified that Lalit Modi's right of residency was not cancelled, since the Enforcement Directorate did not file an extradition request. The Adjournment Motion was subsequently rejected with a voice vote.

### The Minister who brought a Human Touch to MEA

Indian diplomats in overseas missions had taken to sleeping with their cellphones switched on. Sushma Swaraj, the External Affairs Minister (EAM), had the habit of calling—regardless of the time difference—if she got a tweet or heard that an Indian was in distress. "I do not sleep. I do not let Indian envoys sleep," gibed Sushma Swaraj at a press conference once. But it was more than just a light-hearted remark. It was the way she worked. This personalised stamp of diplomacy is what made her the great leader that she was.

There were no interviews for the press. But Sushma Swaraj was available to the aam Indian (general public), even during times of her illness. She once said: "We have worked to integrate people's policy into the foreign policy... Ask those Indians who are stuck in foreign lands." This had been one of her biggest achievements, the transformation of a ministry that so far remained focused on diplomacy—viewed as aloof—to become more people oriented. She became the patron saint of the stranded Indian. It was her efforts which brought back the deaf-mute Gita from Pakistan, and later, Uzma who escaped a bad marriage and captivity. Then there was Gurpreet, the victim of an abusive marriage, who found herself in a German refugee camp. Gurpreet reached out to the minister over social media, and was soon brought home. While these women became Hindustan ki betiyaan, Sushma, gradually changed into the benevolent Bharat Mata herself.

Turning social networking into a powerful tool, Sushma Swaraj quickly won hearts and minds. She tweeted on her own. And despite all the rescue and crisis management she affected over her tweets, she

(The Economic Times)

**Sushma Swaraj with Mute Gita Rescued from Pakistan**

always had time for a joke. Once, someone asked her whether it was safe to travel to Bali, and she tweeted, tongue in cheek, that she would consult the volcano and revert. One of her early tweets to go viral was in response to the annoyed owner of a Samsung refrigerator. She tweeted: "Brother, I cannot help you in matters of refrigerator. I am very busy with human beings in distress."

It was no surprise that Mrs. Swaraj had one of the largest following on social media among politicians. In a country where foreign policy is dominated by the prime minister, she brought something special to the post of EAM.

It was not only the stranded Indian, Sushma Swaraj also facilitated travel permits to many who sought medical visas. In one of her last interventions, she sought information on why German national, Friederike Irina Bruning's visa extension had been denied. Bruning, a Padma Shri, was threatening to return her award. The extension to her student visa was denied due to a technical problem which prevented her from converting her student visa to an employment visa.

In 2016, the Ministry of External Affairs (MEA) generated Twitter Seva Service to ensure that no one is left out. The application tracks the concerns or complaints and redirects it to the official concerned who handles the grievance or the issue concerned, and responds either on Twitter or offline. The first tweet by the new Foreign Minister, S. Jaishankar, assured all Indians, that "Team MEA India" will "continue to be at your service 24x7." And in true form, Jaishankar, appreciated the quick action the Embassy in Riyadh had reached out to a distressed Indian worker who needed to go back home urgently.

Sushma Swaraj knew the names of everyone who worked under her. She was accessible. As one official said, "We know we will get an appointment if we ask." More than her bonds within the ministry, Sushma Swaraj, who had worked for years in Parliament and was skilled at building bridges with the opposition, will be missed by her peers in other countries. On first-name terms with most leaders, she enjoyed a great rapport with them.

Once Mrs. Swaraj told KPS Oli Sharma, Prime Minister of Nepal, that India was the older brother in the neighbourhood. But India was more the caring elder brother or Bade Bhaiya in the relationship, which was very different from the western concept of the bullying Big Brother. As the older sibling, India had the right and responsibility to care for the younger ones. Her successor could take a leaf out of her page in smoothening sharp edges of relationships.

Sushma brought the great Indian family ethos into her work approach. If she was Bharat Mata to the stranded, she was Badi Didi to world leaders younger to her.

Despite failing health, she would take personal interest in everything, even the arrangements for parties hosted by her. She celebrated International Women's Day very ceremoniously, inviting women diplomats, government officers and women in media to be a part of it. She would even oversee the decor and menu herself. And because she was a vegetarian, she would always ask the guests whether the non-vegetarian food was up to the mark. It was one thing she didn't decide.

## Her Path-Breaking Measures

Sushma Swaraj—who was the most followed Foreign Minister in the world—took several path-breaking measures during her term, such as the expansion of the passport infrastructure and the enhanced engagement with the 'Look East policy.'

When Mrs. Swaraj became the second woman External Affairs Minister of India and the first from the Bharatiya Janata Party (BJP), little did the world know that India's diplomacy was going to change forever.

With over 11 million twitter followers in 2018, Sushma Swaraj became the most-followed woman leader in the world. A year later (until the time of her death), she had over 13.1 million followers. But her popularity was not built merely on account of the goodwill she collected from people across borders and boundaries, it was also on the back of being a solid orator, firm socialist and a revered and enthusiastic parliamentarian, which got her the recognition during her long political career.

## Operation Rahat

Operation Rahat was launched by the Indian Armed Forces to evacuate more than 4,000 Indian citizens and other foreign nationals from Yemen during the 2015 military intervention by Saudi Arabia and its allies. The 11-day evacuation by sea started on 1 April, 2015 from Aden port. Even though relentless Saudi bombing of Yemenese locations had made evacuation of Indian civilians very difficult, the operation was successfully carried out. The Saudi king had then said that even though he was unable to bring about a total halt to the bombings, India's request was too important to be ignored.

## How was this possible?

Sushma Swaraj approached the Prime Minister, Narendra Modi and suggested that the excellent rapport he enjoyed with Saudi King (Salman) be put to good use. He, then, made a direct phone call to the King in Riyadh, requesting a safe passage for Indian nationals and sought a halt in bombings for a week.

The Saudi King replied that India's request was too important to be ignored but also expressed his inability in bringing about a total halt to the bombings. The Saudi King, due to his friendship with PM Modi, agreed to halt bombings between 9 AM and 11 AM daily for a week.

Seizing the opportunity, Mrs. Swaraj requested the Yemenese authorities to open their Aden port and airport in Sanaa, so that civilians could be evacuated to Djibouti with alacrity for two hours daily for a week.

This coordination set in motion a critical evacuation exercise of not only 4,800 Indians but also 1,972 people from other countries in 'Operation Rahat' which was led from the front by Minister of State for External Affairs and former Army Chief General (retired) VK Singh.

## Reaching out to people

It was through Twitter that she made the Indian Foreign Ministry—otherwise known as elitist, bureaucratic, distant and indifferent—people friendly, accessible and responsive to the needs of the common people. She was quick to respond when issues were brought to her notice, and she not only helped Indians abroad but people of other nationalities as well–most notably Pakistan when they approached her for help.

With her round-the-clock social media presence and eagerness to help any Indian in distress worldwide, she struck a chord with young and old alike.

In 2015, Neha Agarwal Parikh, an analyst tweeted to help her mother out of Turkey, who was stranded in Istanbul after misplacing her passport. A few hours later, Sushma Swaraj responded asking her to provide her parents' phone numbers. In a short while, the Indian Embassy in Turkey got in touch with her father. "By 6 pm, they had their documents in hand and they boarded the same plane that they were supposed to, a day before," she says. "I am impressed how things moved so fast. Being on Twitter is a good initiative by the government."

A 48-year-old Indian man in Dubai, Jagannathan Selvaraj, who had been living in a public park and had no money for even a bus ticket, had walked more than 1,000 kilometers over two years to attend court proceedings to obtain a flight ticket to return home.

Jagannathan Selvaraj, who hails from Tiruchirappalli, braved traffic, heat, sandstorms and exhaustion after he was denied permission to go back to India to attend his deceased mother's funeral. Sushma Swaraj decided to intervene and sought a report from the Indian consulate in Dubai in 2016.

In 2017, Mrs. Swaraj assured all possible help to an Indian student admitted in a hospital in Georgia, US. She took to Twitter to extend help to the student after she was approached by the latter's sister. In 2018, she assured help to a 14-year-old girl named Isha facing visa issues for her travel to London after being selected to represent India at a global conference.

In 2018, Mrs. Swaraj also assured assistance to a woman who said her brother had gone to Kuwait for some office work and she later lost contact with him. The woman sought Sushma Swaraj's help to locate her brother and shift him back to India. "I have asked Indian Ambassador in Kuwait to provide all assistance," Sushma Swaraj assured the woman.

Later in 2018, she also guaranteed help to a group of Indian students of the University of Illinois in the US who lost their passports in a fire accident. She also extended help to a woman whose passport was stolen while on a trip to Mexico and wanted to get back home as soon as possible as her children were alone.

TV actor Karanvir Bohra, who was stuck at Moscow International Airport thanked her for asking the Indian Embassy in Russia to intervene and for helping him get a temporary passport and a visa for Russia after he was detained at the airport due to passport issues.

In April 2019, Darshan Senthil, a biomedical engineering student wanted to return to India from the US. He applied for an Irish visa, which faced some complications and he asked her for help. Mrs. Swaraj immediately asked the Indian Embassy in the US to help the troubled student.

In April 2019, a civil war broke out in Libya between the Libya National Army and the pro-GNA militias, leaving many Indians stranded in the country amid a volatile situation. Mrs. Swaraj was again quick to help out the people.

After the explosions in Sri Lanka on 21 April 2019, Sushma Swaraj took to twitter to share the helpline numbers and assure every assistance to the distressed and panic-stricken Indians in the Island nation.

In April 2019, a woman asked Sushma Swaraj for help over her husband's distress. He was stranded in Guinea with his passport confiscated for more than one month. Sushma Swaraj asked Y.K. Sailas Thangal, Ambassador of India to the Republic of Cote d'Ivoire, to look into the matter and assured the woman that she has asked for a report from the Ambassador.

In May 2019, five Indian sailors were abducted by pirates in Nigeria. Sushma Swaraj asked the Indian High Commissioner there to take up the matter at the highest level of the Nigerian government to ensure their release. She also asked Abhay Thakur, the Indian Ambassador in Nigeria to look into the matter and send her a report.

## The case of Hamid Ansari

Hamid Nehal Ansari, an Indian spent three years in a Pakistani jail on charges of espionage after being arrested in 2012. The 33-year-old was arrested by intelligence agencies in Pakistan after he allegedly entered northwest Pakistan illegally to meet a woman he met online. He faced trial by military court and was given a three-year sentence in 2015 for possessing a fake Pakistani identity card on December 15, 2015. His jail term ended on December 15, 2018 but he could not leave for India as his legal documents were not ready.

Hamid is a software engineer who suddenly was reported missing after he was taken into custody by Pakistani intelligence agencies and local police in Kohat in Khyber-Pakhtunkhwa. The Peshawar High Court was informed he was in custody of the Pakistan army and was being tried by a military court only after his mother, Fauzia Ansari, filed a *habeas corpus* petition through Pakistani lawyers. Fauzia said: "He went with noble intentions but initially went missing and was later caught and framed. He shouldn't have gone without a visa. His release is a victory for humanity," she told *ANI*.

The External Affairs Ministry had raised the issue of Ansari in a note verbale, or formal communication which was sent to Pakistan on December 11 along with fears that he would be held for almost a month for completion of formalities after his sentence ended on December 15.

Recently, the Peshawar High Court had given a one-month deadline to the Pakistan government to complete formalities for Ansari's repatriation after hearing an appeal filed by his lawyer. After her son's return, Fauzia Ansari couldn't hold her tears. She thanked Sushma Swaraj saying, "meri madam mahaan!" (My madam is great).

## She helped foreign nationals as well

It was not only Indians that Sushma Swaraj came forward to help; in October 2017, when a Pakistani woman named Hira Ahmed appealed to her to approve the pending medical visa request of her one-year-old daughter for her open-heart surgery, she immediately obliged. It was for these gestures, that she was tagged the 'supermom' of India by *The Washington Post.*

## When online trolls came after the affable leader

However, due to her proactiveness on Twitter, even she was not spared by the wrath of trolls. In 2018, Sushma Swaraj and her family were attacked by internet trolls for helping a Muslim couple get their passports. At that time her husband Swaraj Kaushal had jumped to her defence and told them to back off, saying their words had "brought unbearable pain on him" and the family.

Sushma Swaraj's sense of fair play was evident from the way she handled the alleged humiliation faced by an inter-faith couple who complained that a passport office in Lucknow had asked the woman to change her last name and the man to convert to Hinduism. She transferred the official and ensured that the couple's documents were cleared. Later, when she was trolled mercilessly on Twitter for her action in support of the couple, she faced the assault with dignity and carried out a poll against such trolling, where more than half the respondents supported her.

❑

# Chapter-13

## A Foreign Minister with an Impressive Home Connect

Sushma Swaraj was indisputably the most accessible Foreign Affairs Minister the country has ever had. She took full advantage of social media to reach out to people in distress. But her seriousness and commitment towards her job went much beyond her Twitter outreach.

She, as External Affairs Minister, was extremely confident of the important space occupied by India on the global platform and one could not bully her easily. Last year, when the US re-imposed trade sanctions against Iran and warned other countries that they should stop their trade with the country, her initial reaction was one to make all Indians proud.

"India follows only UN sanctions, and not unilateral sanctions by any country," she said at a press conference, and added "that the country will continue to trade with its long-time ally, Iran." Although there was dilution in India's firm position on Iran subsequently, it was likely that this was due to instructions from more powerful quarters within the government.

### A Tall Leader

Her warm demeanour and positive body language was much appreciated by most of the foreign leaders she would meet. As news of her passing away became official, condolence messages poured in from all parts of the world describing her as "a good friend" "a people's person" and a "tall leader."

Due to her ill health she did not contest the last Lok Sabha elections and therefore, could not step in as Minister for External Affairs for the second time. However, she had managed several feathers in her cap in the previous regime. Knowing exactly where the 'wearer knows where the shoe pinches', she launched a new scheme under which a person can apply for a passport from anywhere in India irrespective of their place of stay. She also launched a mobile application available in Android and iOS platforms, that would have the facilities for applying, paying and scheduling appointments for acquiring a passport.

Under the new scheme launched on 26 June, 2018 on the occasion of the Sixth Passport Seva Divas, a person can choose the Regional Passport Office (RPO) and the Passport Seva Kendra (PSK) or Post Office Passport Seva Kendra (POPSK) for submitting the application. The application can be submitted irrespective of whether the person's present residential address was within the jurisdiction of the selected RPO or not. The police verification, if required for a specific passport, would be conducted at the address specified in the application form. The passport will be printed and despatched by the RPO selected for application submission by the applicant to the address specified in the application. For example, a resident of Jaipur, who is temporarily residing in Kolkata, will now be able to apply at a PSK or POPSK under the RPO, Kolkata, and will not have to travel all the way back to Jaipur to submit an application for a passport at a PSK or POPSK under the Jaipur RPO.

Sushma Swaraj was the first Indian to address the Organisation of Islamic Cooperation Summit as a Guest of Honour on March 1, 2019 which was hailed as a major diplomatic victory for India as Pakistan had boycotted the meeting. She also won praise for her successful handling of the crisis in Maldives, India's stand-off with China over Doklam, and Kulbhushan Jadhav's case in the International Court of Justice.

She had also posted a picture with Kulbhushan Jadhav's family which paid a visit to her after the International Court of Justice (ICJ) granted consular access to the former naval officer being tried in Pakistan for alleged spying charges. She reportedly, just an hour before her death, had asked senior advocate Harish Salve to come to her office to collect his Re 1 fee for representing India's case for Jadhav at the international court.

Not just Pakistanis, in 2015, Mrs. Swaraj helped out a Yemeni woman who was married to an Indian. The woman had tweeted an image of her 8-month old baby and made a plea for evacuation from the conflicted area.

For the Foreign Minister who was witty enough to say that if any Indian ever gets stuck on Mars, the Indian Embassy there will help them out, the responsibility was huge, but never a burden. Mrs. Swaraj took decisions from her heart while helping distressed citizens and ensuring that India stood tall on international platforms.

❑

# Chapter-14

## Sushma Swaraj with World Leaders

Sushma Swaraj travelled to 22 countries, 10 of which had been to prepare for prime ministerial visits to those nations, including Nepal, Myanmar, Sri Lanka, the US and China.

The visits resulted in wins for India, both bilaterally and in forums like SAARC, ASEAN and G20. With SAARC, agreements on the long-overdue Motor Vehicles Network and electricity grid were signed. The critical Free Trade Agreement in services with ASEAN, which will benefit Indian professionals in IT and logistics, has seen progress. Critical bilaterals with the US, were finally smooth with little grumbling that was heard from Washington in the past years.

(Reuters)

1. Indian Foreign Minister Sushma Swaraj meets Japan's Prime Minister Shinzo Abe at his official residence in Tokyo, Japan.

2. Sushma Swaraj and Bangladesh Prime Minister Sheikh Hasina at the UN in New York.

(PTI)

3. Sushma Swaraj with Emir of Qatar Sheikh Tamim Bin–Hamad Al-Thani in Doha.

(PTI)

4. Sushma Swaraj shakes hands with Vivian Balakrishnan, Minister of Foreign Affairs of Singapore before a meeting in New Delhi.

(PTI)

5. Former US Secretary of State Hillary Clinton greets India's Foreign Minister Sushma Swaraj in New York.

(Reuters)

6. Russian President Vladimir Putin being received by External Affairs Minister Sushma Swaraj on his arrival in New Delhi.

(PTI)

7. Sushma Swaraj meets Minister for Europe and Foreign Affairs of France Jean-Yves Le Drian, in New Delhi.

(PTI)

8. Sushma Swaraj shakes hands with his Iraqi counterpart, Ibrahim al-Jaafari before a meeting in New Delhi.

(PTI)

9. Sushma Swaraj shakes hands with Chinese Foreign Minister Wang Yi in Beijing, China.

(Reuters)

10. Sushma Swaraj and Foreign Minister of Mongolia Damdin Tsogtbaatar during the 6th India-Mongolia Joint Committee meeting at Ulaanbaatar in Mongolia.

(PTI)

11. Sushma Swaraj shakes hands with Sameh Shoukry Foreign Affairs Minister of Egypt before a meeting in New Delhi.

(PTI)

❑

# Chapter-15

## A Partnership of Equals

Sushma Swaraj, a former Supreme Court lawyer, too had a filmy love story with her husband, Swaraj Kaushal. In fact, their love story began in their college days when she met her husband, a fellow lawyer and friend. Their story became known to everyone when she decided to quit active politics to spend more time with her husband.

Sushma Swaraj and Swaraj Kaushal had met during their college days while studying law in Delhi. Both were believers of diametrically opposite ideologies—Sushma Swaraj was brought up in a political atmosphere as her father was a Rashtriya Swayamsevak Sangh (RSS) member, while Swaraj Kaushal had a socialist belief system.

The two fellow-lawyers worked together with a team of lawyers in the Supreme Court, who contested the George Fernandes case during the days of the Emergency.

(Weddingz)

**Sushma Swaraj and Swaraj Kaushal**

Breaking all odds, Sushma Swaraj dared to marry Swaraj Kaushal during the Emergency period on July 13, 1975. Like every love story, their story too had a filmy twist. Their families had raised objection to their match. As Sushma came from an orthodox Haryana family, getting married to the man of her choice was not an easy task for her. But, fearless Sushma went on to take her husband's name as her surname.

## Her Family Life

A criminal lawyer by profession, Swaraj Kaushal married Sushma Swaraj in July 1975 during the Emergency period. It was only after the Emergency that he joined the Bharatiya Janata Party. He became India's youngest Advocate General at the age of 34. He also served as the Governor of Mizoram from 1990 to 1993. He was also a Member of Parliament from 1998 to 2004. Presently, Swaraj Kaushal serves as a senior advocate with the Supreme Court of India. The couple also has a daughter, Bansuri who is a graduate from Oxford University and a Barrister at Law from Inner Temple.

The couple shared a great camaraderie. Last year, when she announced her decision of not contesting the Lok Sabha elections, Swaraj Kaushal was the happiest and wrote a heartfelt note to her. He expressed gratitude to her for deciding not to contest the Lok Sabha elections. He also compared her to Milkha Singh and said that there was a time when even he had to stop running.

Sushma Swaraj's sister Vandana Sharma is an associate professor of political science in a government college for girls in Haryana. Her brother Dr. Gulshan Sharma is an Ayurveda doctor based in Ambala.

❑

# Chapter-16

## Demise of an Illustrious Leader

Sushma Swaraj, an astute politician and one of India's most popular leaders, passed away on August 6, 2019 after suffering a massive cardiac arrest. The senior BJP leader was brought to the All India Institute of Medical Sciences (AIIMS) around 10 pm and taken to the emergency. While doctors tried to revive her for about an hour, she died at 10.50 pm, the hospital said in its statement. She was 67 years old.

Sushma Swaraj's health had deteriorated lately. She decided to discontinue as India's External Affairs Minister in the new Modi cabinet over health issues. She was known for being an easily accessible and approachable minister and was frequently found helping Indians stranded abroad due to passport and visa issues.

**Sushma Swaraj Passes Away** **(News Nation English)**

(Business Today)

Following the news of her death, politicians, actors, sportsmen, business leaders and other eminent personalities took to Twitter to pay their tributes. She had 13.1 million followers on Twitter. In the last tweet she posted—hours before her untimely death—she congratulated PM Modi for revocation of Article 370. "Thank you Prime Minister. Thank you very much. I was waiting to see this day in my lifetime," she said. At the time of publishing, the tweet had 229.5k likes and 54.7k retweets.

❑

# Chapter-17

## A Glorious Chapter Comes to an End

One of the most prolific politicians of India, her sudden demise triggered a wave of shock and grief with leaders cutting across political spectrum paying glowing tributes to the astute leader.

**President Ram Nath Kovind:** "Extremely shocked to hear of the passing of Smt Sushma Swaraj. The country has lost a much loved leader who epitomised dignity, courage & integrity in public life. Ever willing to help others, she will always be remembered for her service to the people of India."

(The Indian Express)

**Prime Minister Narendra Modi:** "Sushmaji was a prolific orator and outstanding Parliamentarian. She was admired and revered across party lines. She was uncompromising when it came to matters of ideology and interests of the BJP, whose growth she immensely contributed to."

"An excellent administrator, Sushmaji set high standards in every Ministry she handled. She played a key role in bettering India's ties with various nations. As a Minister we also saw her compassionate side, helping fellow Indians who were in distress in any part of the world."

"I can't forget the manner in which Sushmaji worked tirelessly as EAM in the last 5 years. Even when her health was not good, she would do everything possible to do justice to her work and remain up to date with matters of her Ministry. The spirit and commitment was unparalleled."

"Sushmaji's demise is a personal loss. She will be remembered fondly for everything that she's done for India. My thoughts are with her family, supporters and admirers in this very unfortunate hour. Om Shanti."

**Congress leader Rahul Gandhi:** "I'm shocked to hear about the demise of Sushma Swarajji, an extraordinary political leader, a gifted orator & an exceptional Parliamentarian, with friendships across party lines. My condolences to her family in this hour of grief. May her soul rest in peace. Om Shanti."

**Home Minister Amit Shah:** "Deeply saddened by the sudden demise of former External Affairs Minister and senior BJP leader and Member of Parliamentary Board, Mrs. Sushma Swaraj."

Swaraj's death was a great loss not just for BJP but for the entire political landscape of the country. "She was the shining star of our party, she worked tirelessly under guidance of Atalji and Advaniji. She served with dedication in Modiji's 1st term. I am deeply saddened today," he said.

**Defence Minister Rajnath Singh:** "Deeply shocked and anguished by the sudden demise of an extremely valued colleague." In his tribute, he called her the 'People's Minister'.

**External Affairs Minister S. Jaishankar:** "Deeply shocked to learn of the passing away of Smt Sushma Swaraj. Difficult to accept this news. The whole nation grieves, the Foreign Ministry even more so."

**TMC Chief Mamata Banerjee:** "Deeply saddened, shocked at the sudden passing away of Sushma Swarajji. I knew her since the 1990s. Even though our ideologies differed, we shared many cordial times in Parliament. An outstanding politician, leader, good human being. Will miss her. Condolences to her family/admirers."

**Union Minister Smriti Irani:** "I have an axe to grind with you 'Didi.' You made Bansuri pick a restaurant to take me for a celebratory lunch. You left without fulfilling your promise to the two of us."

**Senior party leader Arun Jaitley:** "Pained and broken at her demise. One of the most outstanding politicians in the present era. Swaraj distinguished in all positions she held in the party, the government and the opposition," he said, adding that she leaves behind a void which is difficult to fill.

**Delhi Chief Minster Arvind Kejriwal:** "India has lost a great leader. Sushmaji was a very warm and a remarkable person. May her soul rest in peace."

**Delhi Lt. Governor Anil Baijal:** "Extremely saddened to learn about Sushmaji's tragic untimely departure. A bold, visionary and humane leader, she will sorely be missed by all. May her soul rest in eternal peace."

**Senior Congress leader P. Chidambaram:** "Deeply saddened that Sushma Swarajji has passed away. She served her party and the country with loyalty, devotion and distinction. My sincere and heartfelt condolences to her family and loved ones."

**Congress leader Manish Tewari:** "Absolutely shocked to hear about the passing away of stalwart leader Smt.#SushmaSwaraj! The nation will miss her effervescence, warmth and unmissable receptiveness as a leader!"

**Congress leader Ahmed Patel:** "She was a warm-hearted person, a passionate leader, an excellent orator and a true stateswoman. Her demise has left the country with an irreparable vaccum, it marks the end of an era."

**Leader of the Opposition in the Rajya Sabha, Ghulam Nabi Azad:** "Shocked to hear about the untimely death of sister Sushma Swaraj. She was a great human being and will always be remembered."

**H.D. Deve Gowda:** "I am deeply saddened by the sad demise of former Union Minister, ex-CM of Delhi, Sushma Swarajji. A loss to our Nation. May God give her family the courage to bear this pain." He also wrote to Swaraj Kaushal, husband of late former Union Minister Sushma Swaraj: "My heartfelt condolences to the family. I pray the Almighty to give your benign self, all the family members, followers & well-wishers the strength to overcome this tragedy."

**Karnataka Chief Minister B.S. Yediyurappa:** "Nation mourns today the loss of one of the strongest leaders and finest spokespersons India has seen. Her work as the MEA has been impeccable and as a politician she inspired many women to enter politics. May her soul rest in peace. Om Shanti."

**JD(S) chief H.D. Kumaraswamy:** "I'm shocked to learn about the sudden demise of Former Chief Minister of Delhi, Former Union Minister Sushma Swarajji. May her soul rest in peace. My condolences to her family and loved ones."

**Former Chief Minister Siddaramaiah:** "I am deeply shocked to know that former Foreign Minister Sushma Swaraj is no more."

**Kerala Chief Minister Pinarayi Vijayan** expressed deep condolences on her demise. He hailed the popular leader's contributions in Parliamentary and Diplomatic Affairs Ministries.

**Senior party leader Prakash Javadekar** expressed his shock and said Swaraj set an example by connecting the common man's need to the External Affairs Ministry.

**BJP working president J.P. Nadda:** "Swaraj was an example of an ideal personality, be as an Opposition leader or as External Affairs Minister. Her loss is irreparable and the void left by her can never be filled. It's a huge loss to the party and the nation."

**Law Minister Ravi Shankar Prasad:** "We used to address her as 'didi' and the respect she commanded was phenomenal. She was fine in the morning and then, suddenly, we got this news. It is a painful loss for me and for the nation."

**Senior BJP leader Shahnawaz Hussain** also grieved the loss, saying Swaraj had guided him in his career and "she was a leader liked by everyone, from the ruling to the opposition parties." Her contribution in the External Affairs Ministry is substantial as she left a mark in the field, he said.

**Delhi Deputy Chief Minister Manish Sisodia:** "The news of the passing away of Sushma Swaraj is extremely sad. Her contribution to Indian politics would remain immortal. May her soul rest in peace."

**Telangana Chief Minister K. Chandrasekhar Rao,** through a release from the Chief Minister's Office, praised her services to the nation in different capacities and conveyed his condolences to bereaved family members.

**Maharashtra Chief Minister Devendra Fadnavis** said, she was a dynamic personality and an able administrator. She had exhibited her skills as an excellent Parliamentarian while playing the role of Leader of the Opposition in the Lok Sabha. "We have lost a senior leader and a mentor, but it is also a personal loss for me," he added.

**Uttar Pradesh Chief Minister Yogi Adityanath** said, she was a powerful orator and a person who won the masses with her influence.

**Punjab CM Amarinder Singh:** "Shocked to learn of the sudden demise of @SushmaSwarajji. I will always remember her as a dynamic and sensitive leader with the ability to empathise with the common people. Will miss her. May your soul rest in peace!"

(New Indian Express)

**Uttar Pradesh Governor Anandiben Patel** expressed her profound grief over Swaraj's sudden demise. "Swaraj was a very dedicated leader who played an important role in the country's politics," she said, adding, "with her demise, an era has come to an end."

**Bihar Chief Minister Nitish Kumar:** "The nation is in grief over her demise and will always remember her efforts in the interests of the country and its people. Her death is an irreparable loss. May her soul rest in peace and members of her family find the strength to bear the tragedy."

**Bihar Governor Phagu Chauhan:** Swaraj was known for her "erudition and patriotism," besides being "hugely popular with admirers in all political parties and a source of inspiration for millions of Indians."

## World Leaders Condole Sushma Swaraj's Demise

Leaders from the US, China, Bangladesh, Iran and Singapore condoled the demise of former External Affairs Minister, Sushma Swaraj and recalled her important role in cementing India's relations with the world.

Terming her a "friend" and "strong partner" **US Secretary of State Mike Pompeo** said, Swaraj shared America's view that a more democratic world is a more peaceful one. "Saddened to hear of the passing of my friend and former India External Affairs Minister Sushma Swaraj. She was a strong partner who shared our view that a more democratic world is a more peaceful one. Our thoughts are with her family and the people of India," Pompeo said in a tweet.

In her tribute, **Bangladesh Prime Minister Sheikh Hasina** said her country had lost a "good friend." "She (Swaraj) was a good friend of Bangladesh. With her death, Bangladesh has lost a good friend. Bangladesh will recall her contributions in taking the relationship between the two countries to a new height."

**Iranian Foreign Minister Javad Zarif** recalled his "fruitful" discussions with Swaraj. "My deepest condolences to the government and the people of India on the passing of former External Affairs Minister Sushma Swaraj. I had many fruitful and useful discussions with her while she held office, and am saddened by her sudden passing. May she forever rest in peace," he tweeted.

**Chinese Foreign Ministry spokesperson Hua Chunying** said, Swaraj had made important contributions to the development of China-India relations. "Madam Sushma Swaraj is a senior Indian politician. China deeply mourns for the passing of Madam Sushma Swaraj and expresses sincere condolences to her family."

**Prime Minister Ranil Wickremesinghe** expressed sorrow at the demise of Swaraj, saying that her efforts to achieve regional policy objectives made a lasting impression among the Lankan public. "I have always known Mrs Swaraj as a true friend of Sri Lanka, a neighbour and a relative of Sri Lanka who held a pleasing personality."

**Singapore Foreign Affairs Minister Vivian Balakrishnan** remembered Swaraj's "warm friendship" and said that she represented India on the world stage and fought tirelessly for Indian citizens.

"Sushma Swaraj was a wonderful lady, always full of life, as she represented India on the world stage and fought tirelessly for her citizens," wrote the Singapore minister.

**Bahrain's Foreign Minister Khalid bin Ahmed Al Khalifa** referred to Swaraj as his "dear sister" and said she always called him "My Brother." "She is not with us anymore. Rest in Peace 'my dear sister'. India and Bahrain will miss you," he tweeted.

Paying tributes to Swaraj, the **Russian Foreign Ministry** said on Twitter, "We express our sincere condolences to the people of India on the passing away of the former FM of this friendly country Sushma Swaraj."

The **French Ambassador to India Alexandre Ziegler** said, "she was one of India's most respected leaders who showed remarkable dedication to serving her fellow citizens and took the Indo-French relationship to new heights."

**Israeli Ambassador to India Ron Malka** visited Swaraj's residence and paid his last respects.

Condoling the death of his former Indian counterpart, **Afghanistan's Foreign Minister Salahuddin Rabbani** said, Swaraj led her country with "distinction and determination."

**Foreign Minister of Maldives Abdulla Shahid:** "Deeply grieved to hear the demise of my good friend Smt #SushmaSwaraj; Stateswoman extraordinaire, diplomat par excellence; A warm human being. Key architect of renewed Maldives-India friendship. Sincere condolences to bereaved family and people of India. May she rest in peace!"

**Dean of Diplomatic Corps Hans Dannenberg Castellanos:** "The diplomatic community in Delhi joins the nation in sorrow for the sad demise of a great woman in Indian politics, and one that during her tenure as Foreign Minister strengthened the position of India in the World. We extend our deepest condolences to Mrs. Sushma Swaraj's family and friends."

**UN General Assembly President Maria Fernanda Espinosa:** "Saddened by the news of the passing of @SushmaSwaraj, an extraordinary woman & leader who devoted her life to public service." "I had the honor of meeting her in my visits to #India, & will always remember her fondly. My deepest condolences to all of her loved ones," she added.

**Former Afghanistan President Hamid Karzai:** "Deeply saddened to hear of the loss of 'Behinji' Sushma Swaraj. A tall leader and a great orator and people's person. My profound condolences to the people of India and her family and friends."

❑

# Chapter-18

## Remembering Sushma Swaraj

Many prominent foreign ambassadors and delegates and Heads of States from various countries paid tributes to Sushma Swaraj, remembering her valuable contribution to international diplomacy and strengthening of India's foreign relations.

**The Prime Minister Shri Narendra Modi** remembered former External Affairs Minister, Late Smt Sushma Swaraj on her first death anniversary. He said, "Remembering Sushmaji on her first Punya Tithi. Her untimely and unfortunate demise left many saddened. She served India selflessly and was an articulate voice for India at the world stage."

**Vice President, M Venkaiah Naidu** said that he missed his dear sister, Sushma Swaraj on the occasion of Raksha Bandhan. "Dear sister Sushma, missing you a lot today," along with an old picture of the late BJP leader tying him a 'rakhi.'

Sushma Swaraj's husband **Swaraj Kaushal** wrote a poignant message on Twitter: **"Dil ki naazuk ragein tootati hain, Yaad itanaa bhi koi na aaye, Aaj socha toh aansu bhar aaye..."** (The delicate veins of the heart break, a person should not be missed this much, my eyes are filled with tears as I did today).

**Bansuri tweeted:** "Ma, you are always with me as my strength. Krishna look after my mother!"

**Dr S Jaishankar**, remembered her predecessor, with a collage of pictures from his days in the Foreign Ministry. "Today, more than ever, remember her fondly. Always an inspiration."

**Lok Sabha Speaker Om Birla,** in his homage to Sushma Swaraj said, "...Her dignified and decorous conduct in the House was exemplary. As External Affairs Minister, she made us proud with her remarkable diplomacy. She also took a novel step of assisting people through Social Media."

**Union Minister Ravi Shankar Prasad** wrote, "Will always remember her as a great orator..."

**General VK Singh** said, "Remembering Sushma Swarajji on her first death anniversary. An able leader, a modest colleague & above all an empathetic human being–Sushmaji embodied all these qualities & more. She left an indelible mark on Indian politics. We are thankful to her for all her contributions," he said.

Even **Pakistan's foreign minister Fawad Hussain** remembered Sushma Swaraj "a giant in her own right" while mentioning that he will miss the 'Twitter fights' with her.

Hussain and Swaraj had a Twitter spat in March 2019 over Hindu girls who were allegedly abducted in Pakistan. Tagging a media report on the alleged abduction, she had tweeted: "I have asked Indian High Commissioner in Pakistan to send a report on this. Two Hindu girls abducted on Holi eve in Pakistan's Sindh." To which Hussain had responded: "Mam its Pakistan internal issue and rest assure its not Modi's India where minorities are subjugated, its Imran Khan's Naya Pak where white color of our flag is equally dearer to us. I hope you'll act with same diligence when it comes to rights of Indian Minorities."

However, Mrs. Swaraj was not one to back down. She replied saying: "Mr. Minister, I only asked for a report from Indian High Commissioner in Islamabad about the kidnapping and forced conversion of two minor Hindu girls to Islam. This was enough to make you jittery. This only shows your guilty conscience."

❑

# Chapter-19

## Distinctions and Records

Sushma Swaraj held several unique distinctions and records in her political career that spanned over four decades. Some of them are given below:

### 1. Youngest Cabinet Minister

In 1977, Mrs. Swaraj became the youngest Cabinet Minister. She was only 25 years old. She held the portfolio of education in the Haryana Cabinet.

### 2. First woman Chief Minister of Delhi

Sushma Swaraj became the first woman Chief Minister of Delhi. Her brief period lasted from October 13, 1998 to December 3, 1998.

### 3. First woman Leader of Opposition in Parliament

Breaking all barriers, Sushma Swaraj became the first woman Leader of Opposition in the Parliament in 2019, after replacing her mentor, Lal Krishna Advani.

### 4. First woman Spokesperson of a Political Party

Sushma Swaraj also became the first woman spokesperson of a political party after the Bharatiya Janata Party appointed her as the national spokesperson.

## 5. First full-time woman External Affairs Minister

During the first tenure of PM Modi's government, Sushma Swaraj served as the first full-time Foreign Minister from May 2014 to May 2019.

## 6. Most followed woman Politician on Twitter

In 2018, Sushma Swaraj became the most followed woman politician on Twitter with 11 million followers. Before her untimely demise due to cardiac arrest, she continued to be the most followed woman politician on Twitter with over 12 million followers.

## 7. First Indian to address Organisation of Islamic Cooperation (OIC)

Sushma Swaraj was the first Indian to address the 46th Session of the Organisation of Islamic Cooperation (OIC) meeting as a Guest of Honour in March 2019. It was viewed as a big diplomatic win for India, which came days after the ghastly Pulwama attack on February 14 which claimed the lives of over 40 CRPF jawans.

## 8. *Limca Book of Records*

Sushma Swaraj and her husband Swaraj Kaushal have been credited as the 'Most Distinguished Couple' by *Limca Book of Records* for their achievements and distinctions at a young age.

❑

# Chapter-20

## Awards and Honours

### Best Parliamentarian Award

Sushma Swaraj received the **Best Parliamentarian Award** twice in the years 2008 and 2010. She was the first-ever and the only woman MP to receive the Outstanding Parliamentarian Award. It was instituted in 1995 by Shivraj Patil, who was the Speaker of Lok Sabha from 1991 to 1996.

(Postoast)

(The Diplomat in Spain)

## Grand Cross of Order of Civil Merit

On 19 February 2019, External Affairs Minister Sushma Swaraj accepted the prestigious **Grand Cross of Order of Civil Merit,** which had been conferred by the Spanish government in recognition of India's support in evacuating its citizens from Nepal during the earthquake in 2015.

## Padma Vibhushan

On 26 January, 2020 Sushma Swaraj, was honoured with the Padma Vibhushan, the country's second highest civilian honour after Bharat Ratna, in recognition of her services to public life and as a parliamentarian. 'Padma Vibhushan' the highest Padma award, is given for exceptional and distinguished service.

❑

# Chapter-21

## Places Named After Her

The Government of India renamed two prominent institutions after Sushma Swaraj as an honour to the late External Affairs Minister. The two institutions are the: **Pravasi Bharatiya Kendra** and the **Foreign Service Institute.**

The **Pravasi Bharatiya Kendra** has been renamed as **Sushma Swaraj Bhavan** as the late External Affairs Minister was known for her empathy in reaching out to distressed Indians worldwide. The Pravasi Bharatiya Kendra is a cultural centre which reflects India's connection with its diaspora around the world.

(Jagran Josh)

(fsialumni.gov.in)

The **Foreign Service Institute** has been renamed as **Sushma Swaraj Institute of Foreign Service.** It is an institution where the training of the diplomats takes place.

On February 16 2020, the State Transport Minister, Mool Chand Sharma, named the **Ambala City bus stand** after the late Sushma Swaraj. The bus stand will now be called **'Sushma Swaraj Bus Stand.'**

❑

# Chapter-22

## Her Five Best Speeches

The former External Affairs Minister, Sushma Swaraj was known for her memorable way with words, from poetry duels with former Prime Minister Manmohan Singh to taking on Twitter trolls with zeal and enthusiasm.

One might not have agreed with her remarks on the Babri Masjid and disapproved of her threat to shave off her head if Congress leader, Sonia Gandhi was sworn in as Prime Minister, but there was no denying her skills as an orator.

### 'Tell Us Why The Caravan Was Looted'

One of her most memorable speech was an exchange with Prime Minister Manmohan Singh in 2011, when she was the Leader of the Opposition in the Lok Sabha. He couldn't restrain himself when she used Urdu couplets to allege charges of corruption against the government.

She said: **"Tu idhar udhar ki baat na kar/yeh bata ki kafila kyun luta/hamein rehzano se gila nahin/teri rahbari ka sawaal hai"** (Do not deflect attention by talking of banalities, tell us why the caravan was looted. We don't have any complaints against the passers-by, we are questioning your leadership).

In a departure from his restrained self, he replied, **"Maana ki tere deed ke kaabil nahin hoon main, tu mera shauk dekh, mera intezar dekh"** (I may not be worthy of your attention, but look at my zeal and my perseverance).

## 'Yes, We Are Communal'

A short-lived Atal Bihari Vajpayee government was facing a no-confidence motion in Parliament in 1996. Kenneth Cooper wrote in *The Washington Post* about it: "Vajpayee, considered a moderate within the BJP, gave in after his repeated attempts to soften the party's reputation for religious intolerance and expand its support in Parliament failed."

(The Straits Times)

It was she who rose to his defence and made what has come to be known as the fiercest speech of her career. **"When one Manthara and one Shakuni can keep the likes of Lord Rama and Yudishthir out of their right to rule, then if you take a look around this House, you will find many Mantharas and many Shakunis opposing us, how can we stay in power?"** she said.

She went on to attack those who considered the BJP's ideology communal: "Yes Mr Speaker, we are communal, because we advocate the singing of Vande Mataram, Yes, we are communal, because we fight for the respect of the national flag, we are communal, because we want to abolish Article 370, we are communal, because we want to put an end to discrimination based on caste and creed in this country, yes we are communal, because we want to get the Uniform Civil Code (Saman Nagrik Samhita) implemented in this country."

## 'Terror And Talks Can't Go Together'

Between 2018-19, she made a series of significant speeches about the deteriorating relations between India and Pakistan. One of these was at the 73rd UN General Assembly debate, in response to Pakistan's accusation that India was stalling the dialogue process.

She said, "Those who take innocent human lives in pursuit of war by other means are defenders of inhuman behaviour, not of human rights. Pakistan glorifies killers; it refuses to see the blood of innocents."

She carried the thought forward at the foreign ministers' meet of the **Organisation of Islamic Cooperation** (OIC). Even though she didn't make a direct mention of Pakistan, she was quite clear in her speech: "If we want to save humanity, we must tell the states who provide shelter and funding to terrorists to dismantle the infrastructure of the terrorist camps..."

## 'The 3 AM Tweet Minister'

During her stint as the External Affairs Minister, she began to be described by supporters as the "3 AM tweet minister" who brought a certain accessibility by connecting with people across locations. To a tweet made in jest by a man who claimed to be stuck on Mars, she famously replied: **"Even if you are stuck on the Mars, Indian Embassy will help you."**

## 'I Am Ready To Undergo Any Punishment'

In 2015, she was accused of having lobbied for Lalit Modi, former chief of the Indian Premier League, and a fugitive in Britain, to get a travel visa for his wife's surgery. She denied the accusations and claimed she had only tried to help Lalit Modi's wife on humanitarian grounds. "If it is a crime to help a woman like her, I want to say that I have committed this crime and, standing in this House, I accept my crime before the entire nation. I am ready to undergo any punishment this House may want to give me."

## Parliament Speech on Kulbhushan Jadhav

(The Indian Express)

**Sushma Swaraj with Jadhav's family**

As External Affairs Minister, Sushma Swaraj's work on Kulbhushan Jadhav's case is commendable. She raised the death row issue of the former Indian Navy officer to International Court of Justice. Talking about the developments in the case, she attacked Pakistan government's treatment of Jadhav's wife and mother in Islamabad. She called out 'gross violation' of human rights by Pakistan and said that they used this meeting as an instrument to further their propaganda. "The truth is that both humanity and compassion were missing during the meeting that was arranged on humanitarian and compassionate grounds," she said. "There are not enough words to condemn the same."

❑

# Chapter-23

## From ISRO, Article 370 to Jadeja getting out, to slamming Azam Khan

Sushma Swaraj thanked Prime Minister Narendra Modi on the abrogation of Section 370 in her last tweet, hours before she passed away on Tuesday evening. She had posted a few other tweets on Monday, congratulating Home Minister Amit Shah and the parliamenterians on the passage of the Jammu and Kashmir Reorganisation Bill in the Rajya Sabha.

Her most recent tweets include a congratulatory message to ISRO scientists on the successful launch of Chandrayaan 2. "I salute @Isro scientists for making India a space superpower by successfully launching #Chandrayaan2. I wish the mission a grand success," she wrote.

In another tweet, on 20 July, she had expressed grief on the demise of Congress leader and former Delhi Chief Minister Sheila Dikshit. "I am sorry to know about the sudden demise of Sheila Dixitji. We were opponents in politics but friends in personal life. She was a fine human being. #SheilaDixit," she wrote.

Among most tweets, the tweet that stood out was her sharp criticism of Samajwadi Party MP Azam Khan over his sexist remarks at Rama Devi, who was presiding over the proceedings during a debate on Triple Talaq in Lok Sabha.

She said: "Azam Khan is known for making such statements which prove that he suffers from mental perversion. The statement that he made while addressing a lady Chairperson crossed all limits of decency. He deserves a stringent punishment to preserve the dignity and decorum of the House."

She had also posted a tweet on India's defeat against New Zealand in the Cricket World Cup Semi-Final. "Yes, I was watching the match and was sorry when Jadeja had to leave. Anyway, it is a sport," she wrote.

This last tweet of Sushma Swaraj and the words used by her left scores of her supporters and admirers in shock and grief. "I congratulate the Home Minister Shri @AmitShah ji for his outstanding performance in Rajya Sabha," she tweeted on Monday after the bills on J&K were passed in the Upper House.

❑

# Chapter-24

## Dedication to Work and to Family

While the entire nation has been lauding her virtues as an administrator and a politician, Sushma Swaraj was dedicated to her personal life as she was to her public life. She was a role model in many regards. She broke many glass ceilings as a woman in politics and that too while remaining a dedicated mother and wife. Old interviews from the late 90s have revealed Swaraj Kaushal talking about how she handled the pressures of motherhood while fulfilling her parliamentary duties.

Mrs. Swaraj's impending solutions to international crises were probably foretold by her ability to pacify daughter Bansuri with ice cream whenever she came home late. She would make a stop at India Gate on her way home to pick up ice cream to calm her annoying daughter.

DNA India

Mrs. Swaraj's loving relationship with husband Swaraj Kaushal is an inspiration for many. The couple kept the romance alive through their friendly comments and jokes on Twitter, which won them many fans. He was perhaps the happiest person on Earth when she announced last year that she would not contest the 2019 Lok Sabha elections. Reacting to her decision to retire, Swaraj Kaushal had said, "Thank you very much for your decision not to contest any more elections. I remember there came a time when even Milkha Singh stopped running."

Perhaps, the sweetest thing Swaraj Kaushal said was, "Madam I am running behind you for the last 46 years. I am no longer a 19-year-old. Please, I am also running out of breath. Thank you." Sushma Swaraj reciprocated his affection fully. In an interview to NDTV in 1998, Sushma Swaraj said she would make it a point to have lunch with her husband whenever she was in town. "No matter what my schedule is, I always make it a point to have lunch with my husband," she said.

Explaining how Sushma Swaraj was a complete family woman, Swaraj Kaushal said, "My mother died of cancer in 1993. Sushma was an MP and a former Education Minister. She lived in the hospital for a year. She refused to engage a medical attendant and attended on my dying mother personally."

"Such was her devotion to the family. As per my father's wish, she lit my father's pyre. We adore her," he added.

❑

# Chapter-25

## PTV Interview with Sushma Swaraj

It was Sushma Swaraj's second Pakistan visit in 2002 when Syed Talat Hussein of Pakistan Television (PTV) interviewed her. This time, she went to her neighbourhood nation as India's Information and Broadcasting Minister. The interview went smooth until the Pakistani anchor resorted to Kashmir and tried to corner one of India's best stateswoman on the issue.

**Pakistani anchor:** "Do you mean to say that whatever is happening in Kashmir is ill-bred by Pakistan?

**Sushma Swaraj:** "It will be better by far, if we steer our discussion to other issues. Initially, I told you not to discuss these things because I know that my answers will sound harsh. Your question is quite straight forward but my answer to this question will sound rather curt."

The **Pakistani anchor** went further asking her to give an answer on Kashmir.

In response came **Sushma Swaraj's** schooling of Syed Talat about India's conduct, which went like, "No, I won't. It is a breach of code of conduct to answer curtly while I am a guest here. Besides, it will also be a breach of India's code of conduct. We had better move to some other issue."

The **Pakistani anchor** who appeared hell bent on brandishing his journalistic expertise murmured, "Our act of turning to some other issues will not solve the problem."

Having let any attack go unreplied, **Sushma Swaraj** said: "Problems will surely be solved. The government will sit together. But they will not be solved within thirty minutes as we are sitting here."

Sushma Swaraj is no more but her prowess in moulding unfavourable conditions in favour will remain a lesson for innumerable Indians battling out in their day-to-day life.

❑

# Chapter-26

## Controversies Around Sushma Swaraj

These are some of her controversies in which she was embroiled over the years.

### Lalit Modi's travel papers - June 2015

Sushma Swaraj was in the middle of a dispute after admitting to having helped former Indian Premier League (IPL) chief Lalit Modi procure documents to travel to Portugal on 'humanitarian grounds.' Where the BJP came out in support of her, Congress demanded her resignation. She even faced resentment for having helped Lalit Modi procure documents to travel to Portugal in 2014. Lalit Modi, who is wanted by the Enforcement Directorate for alleged financial impropriety in the money-spinning IPL, stays in London.

### Twitter War - June 2015

Sushma Swaraj reacted angrily to a tweet suggesting she took favours to get her daughter a seat in a medical college through the North East quota. When a Twitter user suggested that she is no stranger to taking and giving favours as her daughter studied through North East quota in a medical college, Sushma impulsively retorted that her daughter is a lawyer and not into medical profession.

### Pushing to declare *Bhagawad Gita* as a National Scripture – 2014

Mrs. Swaraj's decision of declaring *Bhagawad Gita* as a national scripture, sparked a controversy with TMC and Congress coming out with sharp responses. The original request was made by VHP President Ashok Singhal who wanted Prime Minister Narendra Modi to immediately declare the sacred text of Hindus as a national scripture. She seconded it by stating that the respect of a 'national scripture' was already accorded to *Gita* when Prime Minister Modi gifted it to US President Barack Obama during his visit to the country in September 2014.

## Dancing at Gandhi Memorial - 2011

Sushma Swaraj, the then Leader of Opposition sparked a controversy when visuals of her dancing at Mahatma Gandhi's samadhi while on a protest at Rajghat was aired on television channels. The Congress, demanded her resignation while on the other hand, she defended her act saying she was dancing to the tune of patriotic songs to boost the morale of the cadres which is in keeping with the traditions of the party.

## Sushma Swaraj's claim of Mehbooba Mufti praising Narendra Modi - 2011

Sushma Swaraj's claim that PDP president Mehbooba Mufti had praised Narendra Modi's (then Gujarat CM) work ethics triggered a verbal duel between Mufti and Jammu and Kashmir, Chief Minister Omar Abdullah. Mehbooba Mufti denied reports of her praise of Modi at a recent meeting of the National Integration Council in Delhi and said her remarks were quoted out of context. She asked the Centre to release the transcript of her speech to clear the misgivings.

❑

# Chapter- 27

## Poetry in Parliament

The former External Affairs Minister was not only known for her magnificent work and oratory but was also honoured in the country for standing with all those who needed her. In her party, she was known as a guiding force, and in her political career she was recalled for her political punches. Across party lines, she was honoured not only for being an able administrator, fiery speaker, but also as one who respects her opponents. Her poetic exchanges in the Parliament were a visual treat.

1. In 2013, the then Prime Minister Manmohan Singh used an Urdu couplet to accuse the BJP and then Leader of Opposition Sushma Swaraj of not supporting the government. She also responded using verse of Hindi poet Bashir Badr and declared that the party's compulsion was that Manmohan Singh was disloyal to the nation and that's why it cannot be loyal to him.

   **Manmohan Singh** said: **"Humko hai unse wafa ki umeed, jo nahi jaante wafa kya hai"** (We hope for loyalty from those who do not know the meaning of the word), the Prime Minister quoted famous Urdu poet, Mirza Ghalib.

   In response, **Sushma Swaraj** said: **"Kuch to majbooriya rahi hongi yun koi bewafa nahi hota"** (There must have been some compulsions, one is not disloyal for no reason at all).

   She then broke into a second verse: **"Tumhe wafa yaad nahee, Humein jafa yaad nahee, Zindagi or maut ke toh do hee tarane hain, ek tumhein yaad nahee, ek humein yaad naheen"**

(You don't remember loyalty, we don't remember disloyalty, life and death have two rhythms, you don't remember one, we don't remember the other).

2. While debating the **Street Vendors Protection of Livelihood and Regulation of Street Vending Bill in 2013,** Sushma Swaraj, within thumping of desk from all parts of the house had said that one should think for those who are leading their lives in compulsions.

**"Kisi majbur ki majburiyo ko sochkar dekho**
**Prem ko in jhopadiyo ke bich khojkar dekho**
**Agar insaniyat ko fir se dharti par bulate ho**
**Kisi rote hue ke aansu pochkar dekho**
**Kisi rote hue ke aansu pochkar dekho."**

(Try to think of the helplessness of the helpless
Try to find love amidst these shacks
If you want humanity on this planet
Try to wipe away somebody's tears
Try to wipe away somebody's tears).

3. In 2012, while debating the **Copyright Amendment Bill**, Sushma Swaraj narrated the following:

**"Dost gamkhvari mein meri sai farmavenge kya**
**Zakhm ke bharne talak nakhun na badh javenge kya**
**Hai ab is mamure mein kahat-e-gam-e-ulfat asad**
**Hum ne ye mana ki dilli mein rahe khavenge kya"**

(In my state of sorrow, what help would my friend attempt to administer.
By the time my wounds fill up and heal, wouldn't my fingernails grow up again.
There is now in this place, a drought or scarcity of the grief of love, Asad!
We have agreed to this that we will remain in Dilli, but what will we eat here when there is no passion or love left?)

4. Criticizing the then government over **Bhopal Gas Tragedy** in 2011, Sushma Swaraj concluded her fiery speech with these couplets:

**"Dekhe is Bharat me kaun bada vir balidani hai**
**Kiski dhamni mein khoon aur kiski dhami mein pani hai."**

(Let us see who is the greatest sacrificial hero in India
Let us see whose arteries have blood and whose has water.)

❑

# Chapter-28

## An Effective and Successful Leader

### Personal Initiative

Apart from giving time to India's major foreign policy issues, Sushma Swaraj went out of her way to personally help many distressed citizens. She used her twitter account to help and contact those in need. The most recent example was her promise to extend the visas of a British couple in Mumbai, so that they could wait for the UK to issue their daughter, Lily a passport, who was born through surrogacy in India.

### Quick to take Action

When someone asked her for help, Mrs. Swaraj was quick to reply. Madhu, a migrant girl from Pakistan was finding it difficult to obtain admission in an Indian school as she did not have her previous School Leaving Certificate or Birth Certificate from Pakistan with her. She helped resolve the matter and Madhu was granted admission at a government school.

### Hard Working and Result-Oriented

Sushma Swaraj constantly looked for areas of improvement. She realized that there was a lack of data on Indian students studying abroad, so she implemented a Students Registration module to track these numbers.

### Determined and Resilient

When Mrs. Swaraj was the Minister of Telecommunications, under the

Atal Bihari Vajpayee government in 1998, she declared film production as an 'industry' thereby opening it up to institutional finance, and releasing it from the clutches of loan.

## Empathy

Even when Mrs. Swaraj could not help somebody, she acknowledged them and their problems. When people thanked her, she said that she did not need thanks, and that "it is [her] duty towards our country and countrymen." After wrestler, Vinesh Phogat, suffered from a ligament tear prompting her to drop out from the Rio Olympics quarter final wrestling match, she reached out to her and offered her much needed words of comfort. "Vinesh-you are our daughter. Ask for anything you require," she said.

## Good Communicator

Apart from maintaining an active online presence, Sushma Swaraj was known for her diplomatic skills and follow-up. She held round-table meetings with Indian heads of missions to SAARC, ASEAN and Middle East after taking her position. She spoke fluent Hindi and English and was unabashed as the Leader of the Opposition in the Lok Sabha. In 1999, she competed against Sonia Gandhi from Bellary, and even learned how to speak Kannada.

## Rescue Missions

Sushma Swaraj's ministry rescued 168 Indians who were held hostage in Basra, Iraq. They also rescued 4,640 Indians from Yemen during the Yemeni Crisis in 2015. Many countries also sought India's help to rescue their nationals, and the Indian Armed Forces and the Ministry of External Affairs also rescued 960 foreign nationals. She was responsible for repatriating many other Indians from abysmal situations abroad.

## The Opposition Acknowledged her Work

**Aam Aadmi Party's** Bhagwat Mann, and Dharamveer Gandhi thanked Sushma Swaraj, saying that she was doing a good job in her rescue missions for Indians abroad.

## Her Sense of Humour

Throughout her work, Mrs. Swaraj managed to maintain a positive, and a light-hearted attitude which drew more people to her. Her twitters were very interesting: "I would have definitely joined the Army. But at that time women were not allowed in the armed forces. Now, they say I am overage."

And when someone asked her to help with their refrigerator problems, she wittily replied, "Brother I cannot help you in matters of a Refrigerator. I am very busy with human beings in distress."

❑

# Chapter-29

## Inspirational Sayings

**Reform Must Begin Today;**
**Tomorrow Could Be Too Late.**

**Ek Doosre Ko Dosha-Ropan Karke Kisi Bhi**
**Samasya Ka Samadhan Nahi Ho Sakta,**
**Balki Ek Saath Hokar Hota Hai.**

By blaming each other no problem is ever solved
rather it happens when we are together.

**If We Have to Save the World from the Adverse**
**Effects of Climate Change,**
**Then Developed Nations Must Lift the Deprived**
**with Financial and Technical Resources.**

**Duniya Ki Sabse Badi Se Badi Samasya Ka**
**Samadhan Hota Toh Sirf Sanwaad Se Hi Hai,**
**Yuddh Kisi Bhi Samasya Ka Samadhan Nahi Hai.**

World's biggest problem
Are solved only through dialogue
War is not the solution to any problem.

# Chapter-30

## Surrogacy Bill, 2016

The Surrogacy Regulation Bill, which was cleared by the Union Cabinet on August 24, 2016 for introduction in Parliament seeks not only to "prohibit commercial surrogacy" but also prevents single people, those from LGBTQ community and those in a live-in partnership from experiencing parenthood through surrogacy.

After the meeting, Sushma Swaraj announced: "A draft bill which aims to safeguard the rights of surrogate mothers and make parentage of such children legal has been cleared by the Union Cabinet." She said: "This Bill will prohibit commercial surrogacy and allow ethical surrogacy to needy infertile couples."

What she meant by "ethical surrogacy" was not clarified, but as far as "altruistic surrogacy" is concerned, it's like a movie, that is all in the family.

Not only does it prohibit commercial surrogacy, thereby blocking out possible consensual livelihood options for some women, but it also restricts the ambit of surrogacy within India, only to married Indian heterosexual couples, ostensibly for the sake of transparency and legality.

She went a step further by saying that celebs who take to surrogacy despite having children or despite being unmarried, are indulging in "unethical practices." She lashed out at celebrities for opting for surrogacy saying it has become a trend.

"Big celebrities who not only have one but two children, a son and a daughter, even then they went ahead with surrogacy," said the

Minister. She said: "What was started for convenience has become a luxury today."

Evidently, this was to stop India from being the surrogacy hub for couples abroad, especially non-Indian, rich, white Euro-Americans, for whom India (and China) are one-stop surrogacy destination, leading to unethical medical practices during child-bearing.

But the most exclusionary thrust of the Bill was its rampant bigotry and bias against unmarried, homosexual Indians, or those who are in live-in partnerships, choosing not to get married. She said, "You can say it is looking forward and we can say this doesn't go with our ethos."

Moreover, the wait for married couples would be at least five years, and even NRIs and OCIs will not be allowed to take the surrogacy route to parenthood.

❑

# Chapter-31

## An Epitome of Woman Empowerment

The former External Affairs Minister, was a symbol of women empowerment. She always encouraged women, and the following statement proved that, "We have known IT professionals who hand over their salaries to their mothers-in-law or others who are abused. But a lady police officer's women peon may not have to face all this as troubling her can lead the culprit to jail. This is political empowerment. She said: For us women in politics, our authority moves forward to our women workers and empowers them."

Once in a workshop organised by the BJP Mahila Morcha and Good Governance Cell she said, "Both education and economic independence are important but political empowerment is a higher form of empowerment."

She expressed her views regarding the unfair prejudice in political establishments that women were not winnable candidates and encouraged women by saying that this ideology have been defied by several examples in the present society.

In 2014, turning to the issue of women's empowerment, she said the passage of the women's reservation bill should become the milestone for the 16th Lok Sabha. On November 2017, during Ivanka Trump's visit to India more than half the participants at the Global Entrepreneurship Summit (GES) in Hyderabad were women. Just ahead of the inaugural ceremony of the summit, she met Ivanka. The theme of the conference was "Women First, Prosperity for All." This showed how she uplifted women empowerment being the inspiration for many.

# Chapter-32

## On Gender Equality

"Men should be encouraged to study home science in college and hone their culinary skills, while women should be motivated to take up physical education, especially martial arts, as an effort to banish gender bias from society."

This comment of Sushma Swaraj had created an uproar in the Parliament. For the first time a prominent MP, holding one of the most important portfolios in the government had spoken about gender equality and the need for men to be part of women's lives through the roles they perform. Mothers, wives and young women who already considered her a remarkable woman, now saw her in a new light. That of a real person who talked of real issues that matter to women. Even men sat up and took notice, as here was a leader who was popular and respected beyond the constraint of gender.

She believed that it's necessary for men to learn kitchen skills to ease the burden on women. She raised these issues at a meeting on National Policy for Women in 2017, and asked everyone to question gender stereotypes, starting with the gendered division of labour at home.

In July 2018, when still the Minister of External Affairs, she faced a lot of abuse at the hands of trolls. One man tweeted to her husband, the former Governor of Mizoram, Swaraj Kaushal, that he should beat his wife when she gets back home and "teach her not to do appeasement." All this hatred towards one of the most respected politicians in the country was because the External Affairs Ministry's had granted a passport to an interfaith couple (who had allegedly applied with incomplete documentation) and transferring the official without holding a proper inquiry (after the couple claimed facing religious discrimination from him).

Swaraj Kaushal, the ex-governor came forward in defence of his wife and criticised the hate she had been facing on social media. "Your words have given us unbearable pain. Just to share with you, my mother died of cancer in 1993. Sushma was an MP and a former Education Minister. She lived in the hospital for a year. She refused to engage a medical attendant and attended on my dying mother personally."

Sushma Swaraj was no less a feminist. She used her position of power to remind fellow politicians that women in India were on a movement and that the 'Andolan' was now unstoppable. In 2018, during a **Women's Day** talk in the Parliament, she spelled out the need for India to take notice of women's needs and demands. She hailed India for long having a female Prime Minister and President while developed economies were far behind. But she added, there was need to do more. And, that too with a political will.

❑

# Chapter-33

## Through Bansuri Swaraj's Eyes

Bansuri Swaraj recalled how her mother used to be active on the micro-blogging site and would always say that it was a "celebration of democracy." She added that her mother used to "literally" draft every tweet "meticulously."

"She used Twitter I think very effectively for two things, one for putting her point of view across and second for ensuring she was helping Indians all across the globe," Bansuri said.

Bansuri Swaraj, an advocate with the Supreme Court, shared a video which highlights the bond that she shared with her mother.

(India TV News)

**Sushma Swaraj and daughter Bansuri**

She introduced herself saying, "I am blessed to be Sushma Swaraj's daughter." "There was not a secret kept from her and she did not miss a single report card. My entire life she did not miss a single PTA…I really wish she was here for this as well," she added. She even explained how she followed her mother's footsteps and became an advocate.

She recalled a "heart wrenching" incident where an Indian woman went to the UK but was abandoned by her travel agent in a refugee camp in Germany along with her 8-year-old daughter. The woman made a video and it was tweeted and Sushma Swaraj was tagged. "Within one hour, of that tweet, my mother started working towards bringing her back home," she said.

When asked to describe her mother Sushma Swaraj in five words, Bansuri got emotional. "This is a tough one. Amazing, awe-inspiring, innocent, fearless, and I would say missed."

## Bansuri Remembers Mom on Mother's Day

May 10 marks Mother's Day 2020 and people are posting emotional and heartwarming letters for their mothers on social media. Even Bansuri Swaraj, daughter of India's former External Affairs Minister, who died last year, took to Twitter to remember her mother. Bansuri tweeted, "Happy Mother's Day @SushmaSwaraj. Miss you with every breath Ma." She also shared a 'throwback' picture of her and Sushma Swaraj.

## Bansuri Remembers Parent's Wedding Anniversary

Remembering her mother on the wedding anniversary of her parents, Bansuri Swaraj took to Twitter to express her love and gratitude for her mother, late Sushma Swaraj. While wishing her mom and dad on their special day, Bansuri Swaraj shared a sweet yet simple picture with an emotional caption that left many teary-eyed.

Sharing a black and white picture of her parents from their younger days, Bansuri wrote, "On this date in 1975 Sushma and Swaraj became Sushma Swaraj." She further said, "Happy wedding anniversary Ma and Papa." Bansuri also tagged her mother, late Sushma Swaraj, and father Swaraj Kaushal.

Besides Bansuri, Sushma Swaraj's husband Swaraj Kaushal also shared a post remembering his wife on their special day. In a series of tweets, Swaraj Kaushal showered praises on his late wife for her many accomplishments. In one of the tweets, he said that Sushma became the youngest Cabinet Minister in the country at 25 and state president of the party at 27.

On July 12, Bansuri Swaraj took to Twitter to wish her dad Swaraj Kaushal on his birthday. Sharing a picture of her dad Bansuri wrote, "You are my mother's world and your daughter's pride."

In her passing away, the BJP and Indian politics lost a leader who was not just a powerful orator but also one who was humane, sensitive and approachable to the common person. In many ways, Sushma Swaraj's political journey is the journey of a woman who broke glass ceilings, one by one, to exemplify how women too can excel in politics--an arena traditionally dominated by men.

The people to whose rescue she came were not just Indians across the world but also foreigners who wanted to come to India to seek medical treatment. Whether it was an Indian NGO worker in Kabul, a Christian priest in Yemen or a physically-challenged girl who had wandered into Pakistan, she was there for them all.

Despite her failing health, for which she had to undergo a kidney transplant, her energy levels were high. She remembered people she had met years before, and had absolutely no airs about her.

Her demise has left a major void in Indian politics, that may be difficult to fill for a long time to come.

❑

www.ingramcontent.com/pod-product-compliance
Ingram Content Group UK Ltd.
Pitfield, Milton Keynes, MK11 3LW, UK
UKHW041944080925
7790UKWH00030B/590

9 789390 697069